The Satanic War on the Christian Vol.1 The Reality of Satan & Demons

FIRST PRINTING

Billy Crone

Copyright © 2018
All Rights Reserved

Cover Design:
CHRIS TAYLOR

To my sister, Heather.

*If ever there was two people,
who knew firsthand
the ravages of spiritual warfare,
It would be you and me.*

*Prior to salvation,
both of us,
at various times,
have danced with the devils,
played their games,
and sang their songs.*

*We ingested their poison,
believed their lies,
and even tried to end these lives,
multiple times.*

*But God did what only He can do.
He rescued us from the dominion of darkness,
He saved us from the clutches of the evil one.
He set us free through Jesus Christ.*

*Thank you for not only putting up with me,
and for being a wonderful sister here on earth,
but for now, being a fellow soldier of Christ,
fighting the good fight,
in this greatest battle of all,
The Satanic War on the Christian.*

*Don't ever give up Heather,
We know who wins.*

I love you.

Contents

Preface..vii

PART 1:   **The Reality of Satan & Demons**

1. *The Existence of Satan*..11
2. *The Existence of Demons*..31
3. *The Character of Satan*.. 49
4. *The Character of Demons*...69
5. *The Tactic of Satan*..89
6. *The Tactic of Demons*..107

PART 2:   **The Destruction from Satan & Demons**

7. *The Destruction of the Casual Christian*..Vol.2
8. *The Destruction of the Cultural Christian*..................................... Vol.2
9. *The Destruction of the Compromising Christian*......................... Vol.2
10. *The Destruction of the Corruptive Christian*............................. Vol.2
11. *The Destruction of the Doubting Christian*............................... Vol.2
12. *The Destruction of the Depressing Christian*............................Vol.2

PART 3:   **The Temptation from Satan & Demons**

13. *The Temptation of the Twisted Christian Part 1*........................ Vol.3
14. *The Temptation of the Twisted Christian Part 2*........................ Vol.3
15. *The Temptation of the Tormented Christian Part 1*..................... Vol.3
16. *The Temptation of the Tormented Christian Part 2*..................... Vol.3
17. *The Temptation of the Troubled Christian*................................Vol.3
18. *The Temptation of the Terrified Christian Part 1*....................... Vol.3
19. *The Temptation of the Terrified Christian Part 2*....................... Vol.3
20. *The Temptation of the Traitorous Christian*...............................Vol.3

PART 4:   **The Protection against Satan & Demons**

21. *The Protection from satan & demons Part 1*............................ Vol.4

22. *The Protection from satan & demons Part 2*............................ Vol.4
23. *The Protection from satan & demons Part 3*............................ Vol.4
24. *The Protection from satan & demons Part 4*............................ Vol.4
25. *The Protection from satan & demons Part 5*............................ Vol.4
26. *The Protection from satan & demons Part 6*............................ Vol.4
27. *The Protection from satan & demons Part 7*............................ Vol.4
28. *The Protection from satan & demons Part 8*............................ Vol.4
29. *The Protection from satan & demons Part 9*............................ Vol.4
30. *The Protection from satan & demons Part 10*.......................... Vol.4

How to Receive Jesus Christ........................ 127
Notes... 129

Preface

Why are so few Churches making an impact on the world today? Why are so many believers living defeated lives? Why do so many Christians talk about having a victorious Christian life, yet so few seldom ever do? The answer lies in the greatest spiritual war of all time, The Satanic War on the Christian.

But we have a problem, a big problem in the Church today. You see, you would think that the knowledge and mastery of spiritual warfare would be commonplace among the Christian community. After all, our Lord Jesus Christ took on and defeated the devil himself. But unfortunately, waging war against the enemy of our souls is one of the least talked about topics in the Church today, for a couple of reasons. One reason is because some in the Church have detrimentally taken spiritual warfare to an unhealthy extreme. The result is that the moment you try to talk about spiritual warfare in Christian circles, most people think you're some sort of a weird lunatic. Then, as if that wasn't bad enough, we have the second extreme to deal with. Well over half of all professing Christians today don't even believe that our greatest archenemy, the devil, even exists. No wonder we're losing the fight! Yet in the midst of our sad skepticism, spiritual warfare really is something we all have to deal with every single day here on earth. And unless we get a proper balanced handle on it, we will simply continue to be beaten to shreds spiritually.

Thus, I have written this book, without all the hyper fanaticism, showy sensationalism, or dry theological jargon and simply focused on getting down to the nuts and bolts of the greatest war of all time, the war against the children of God and the forces of hell. It is penned with a powerful concoction of practical information and personal application for personal victory, while clearly exposing the lies, traps, and pitfalls of the very forces of evil. It is my prayer that this book will not only clearly unveil this deadly invisible war and expose the seductive weapons the devil uses to keep the Church from becoming a mighty army for God, but that it will also provide the practical tools needed for the personal spiritual victory that our Lord Jesus Christ has already won for us.

One last piece of advice. When you are through reading this book then will you please READ YOUR BIBLE? I mean that in the nicest possible way. Enjoy, and I'm looking forward to seeing you someday!

Billy Crone
Las Vegas, Nevada
2018

Part I
___

The Reality of Satan & Demons

Chapter One

The Existence of Satan

"It's been the topic of many films, TV shows, songs, books and even computer games. Its code name was Operation Overlord. It happened during WWII. It was the largest amphibious invasion in history with Twelve Allied nations providing the fighting forces. The invasion fleet was drawn from eight different navies comprised of 6,939 vessels, 1,213 warships, 4,126 transport vessels, 736 ancillary craft, 864 merchant vessels, 13,000 fighter, bomber, and transport aircraft, 570,000 tons of supplies, and one million men by the end of the month. Yet, even with such a massive historical invasion, it totally caught the Germans off guard. Some troops stood down. Many of their senior officers were away for the weekend while dozens of divisions, regimental and battalion commanders were away from their posts conducting war

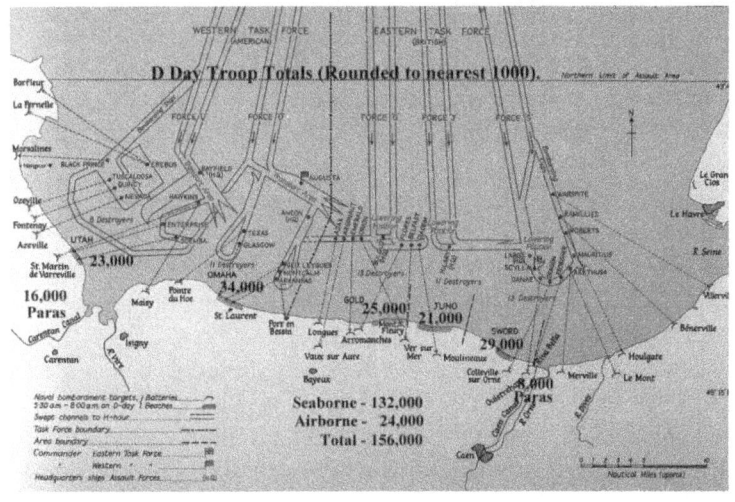

games elsewhere. In fact, one of their most famous generals took a few days' leave to celebrate his wife's birthday. But when all was said and done, on that fateful day, the massive horde of Allied forces invaded the beaches dropping 195,000 tons of bombs and established a beachhead that not only liberated all of northern France but became the beginning of the end for the Nazi Reich. The date was June 6, 1944. The battle was D-Day or the Battle of Normandy."[1]

Now, how many of you have heard of the Battle of Normandy or D-Day? I think we all have. And how many of you guys would say that storming the beaches of Normandy was pretty intense for those men? But with all due respect, to those who lost their lives on D-Day, what if I were to tell you that I know of a battle that makes D-Day look like a birthday party? And what if I were to tell you that this battle didn't occur in just one place and one country at one time, but it's going on right now today all over the world and it's been leaving a trail of death and destruction for centuries. I'm talking about the *Satanic War on the Christian.*

People, these are the facts. We Christians don't battle here and there once in a while. We go to war, every single day. Whether you see it, feel it, believe it or not, the moment you got saved you entered a spiritual war against a demonic host whose sole purpose is to destroy you and extinguish your testimony for Jesus Christ. And what's wild is that most wars go on for a few years or even longer. But the *Satanic War on the Christian* has been going on for the last 2,000 years non-stop and it's sending people straight into hell! And what's wild is most people will readily talk about all the other wars throughout history and all their atrocities, and rightly so, we have the History Channel, we need to talk about them! YET how many people, even Christians, will openly discuss the longest war in mankind's history, the *Satanic War on the Christian,* that has destroyed more lives in all eternity than all the wars put together? Therefore, I don't know about you, but I think it would be wise for us to learn a little bit more about This *Satanic War on the Christian*, how about you guys? Hey, great answer! We're going to do it anyway!

It's pretty simple, if you're ever going to win a war, then the first thing you must do is know who your enemy is, amen? It's common sense, right? And that enemy, is none other than the devil himself. He really does exist, contrary to popular opinion!

Matthew 4:1-11 "Then Jesus was led by the Spirit into the desert to be tempted by the devil. After fasting forty days and forty nights, He was hungry. The tempter came to Him and said, 'If you are the Son of God, tell these stones to become bread.' Jesus answered, 'It is written: 'Man does not live on bread alone, but on every word that comes from the mouth of God." Then the devil took Him to the holy city and had Him stand on the highest point of the temple. 'If you are the Son of God,' he said, 'throw yourself down'. For it is written: 'He will command his angels concerning you, and they will lift you up in their hands, so that you will not strike your foot against a stone." Jesus answered him, 'It is also written: 'Do not put the Lord your God to the test." Again, the devil took Him to a very high mountain and showed Him all the kingdoms of the world and their splendor. 'All this I will give you,' he said, 'if you will bow down and worship me.' Jesus said to him, 'Away from me, satan! For it is written:' Worship the Lord your God and serve him only. Then the devil left Him, and angels came and attended Him."

Now, maybe it's just me, but I'm kind of thinking that the devil, according to the Bible, really does exist and he really tempted Jesus! Anybody else coming to the same conclusion? He's not only mentioned once, not twice, but five times in just eleven from Jesus! Four as the devil, one as satan. But this is the problem! The Church today is losing the *Satanic War on the Christian* because they don't even know who the enemy is! The reason why they don't know who the enemy is, is because they don't believe he exists in the first place. It's crazy, we just read in one passage dealing with our Lord and Savior Jesus, but they say 'Oh no, it's just a figment of your imagination, even though the Bible is extremely emphatic about it!! Don't believe me? Let me share with you some proof:

- *Polls tend to show that Americans consider themselves largely a religious people, with something close to 95% claiming a belief in God. (Now religion doesn't save you. What did Jesus say to those who were into religion? 'Away from me you evil doers, I never knew you.' Going to church services doesn't save you, getting dunked in water doesn't save you, it's only bowing the knee, acknowledging that it is only the work of Jesus Christ on the cross that gives you forgiveness of your sins. That's it! They consider themselves religious. 95% are claiming to believe in God. Now does that save you? No. James Chapter 2 says even the demons believe in God and they shudder. They obviously are not saved.)*

- *In fact, there are also large numbers of Americans saying that they think that Heaven exists, and so do angels. (Now what's ironic is…what is Satan? He's a fallen angel, right? They believe in angels, but only the good ones, so to speak.)*

- *But in another survey people were asked whether they thought hell existed as an actual location, "a place of physical torment'" and only 31% said they thought it did which means 69% said no. (Did you know that hell is a real place and that you are going there unless you call upon the Name of Jesus Christ and ask Him to forgive you of all your sins? He's the only way to get to Heaven.)*

- *And as far as so-called American Christians and their belief in Satan only 35% said he is real which means 65% said he's not, he's just "a mere symbol of evil."*

- *As to the reason why one researcher stated, "Hollywood has made evil accessible and tame, making Satan and demons less worrisome than the Bible suggests they really are," he said. "It's hard for achievement-driven, self-reliant, independent people to believe that their lives can be impacted by unseen forces."*

- *In fact, the results may even be worse than that. On the View, Barbara Walters is quoting a report from a research group. "It divides people into ages and it says only 1% of the youngest adults ages 18-23 has a Biblical world view which is that the Bible is completely accurate, and Satan is a real being. Only 1% of young adults and only 9% of all American adults have a Biblical World view, that is that the Bible is completely accurate which includes Satan being a real being or force."*[2]

So now you're in the upwards of 91-99% who don't believe in the devil! Wow! We're in a heap of trouble! No wonder we don't know who the enemy is, in the Church, we don't even believe he exists! Those statistics are not only mind-blowing, but they're totally unbiblical in light of our text! Jesus was not tempted by "a mere symbol of evil," he was tempted by a literal devil. I didn't say that, Jesus did, multiple times! And what's wild is, you don't have to go very far to find plenty of proof of a literal devil:

"A mother and daughter are driving in the car. The little girl is smiling in the back seat drawing a picture. All of a sudden there is a siren and lights flashing behind them and a policeman pulls her over.

"Good afternoon madam, can I see your papers please?" asks the policeman.

As she is reaching into her purse he notices the little girl in the back seat. "Hello, Mommy was in a bit of a hurry, wasn't she?" He asked her. Very seriously the little girl looks at the policeman and whispers "That's not my mommy." He now pays special attention to what the little girl is saying as she holds up a sign that says 'Help'.

He immediately stands back from the car and yells at the woman, "Step out of the car, now!"[3]

Somebody's in trouble! Wow! Kids can sometimes act like the devil. Okay. But seriously folks, as tempting as those proofs of the devil are, I think there's even more reliable evidence showing us the existence of an actual devil.

The **first and primary source** proving satan's existence is **The Biblical Proof**.

Believe it or not, Matthew 4 is just one of many passages in the Bible showing us and proving the existence of a literal satan, over and over again, in whom we really have to deal with. There really is a war going on! Old Testament, New Testament, he is mentioned all over the place. And so, let's take a look at some of that proof:

Genesis 3:3-5 "The serpent said to the woman, 'You surely will not die! For God knows that in the day you eat from it your eyes will be opened, and you will be like God, knowing good and evil.'"

1 Chronicles 21:1 "Satan rose up against Israel and incited David to take a census of Israel."

Job 1:6-12 "One day the angels came to present themselves before the LORD, and satan also came with them. The LORD said to satan, 'Where have you come from?' satan answered the LORD, 'From roaming through the earth and going back and forth in it.' Then the LORD said to satan, 'Have you considered my servant Job? There is no one on earth like him; he is blameless and upright, a man who fears God and shuns evil.' 'Does Job fear God for nothing?' satan replied. 'Have you not put a hedge around him and his household and everything he has? You have blessed the work of his hands, so that his flocks and herds are spread throughout the land. But stretch out your hand and strike everything he has, and he will surely curse you to your face.' The LORD said to satan, 'Very well, then, everything he has is in your hands, but on the man himself do not lay a finger.' Then satan went out from the presence of the LORD."

Zechariah 3:1-2 "Then he showed me Joshua the high priest standing before the angel of the LORD, and satan standing at his right side to accuse him. The LORD said to satan, 'The LORD rebuke you, satan! The LORD, who has chosen Jerusalem, rebuke you!'"

Matthew 5:37 "Simply let your 'Yes' be 'Yes,' and your 'No,' 'No'; anything beyond this comes from the evil one."

Matthew 6:13 "And lead us not into temptation but deliver us from the evil one."

Matthew 13:19 "When anyone hears the word of the kingdom and does not understand it, the evil one comes and snatches away what has been sown in his heart."

Matthew 16:23 "Jesus turned and said to Peter, 'Get behind me, satan! You are a stumbling block to Me; you do not have in mind the things of God, but the things of men."

John 8:44 "You are of your father the devil, and you want to do the desires of your father. He was a murderer from the beginning and does not stand in the truth because there is no truth in him. Whenever he speaks a lie, he speaks from his own nature, for he is a liar and the father of lies."

John 17:15 "I do not ask You to take them out of the world, but to keep them from the evil one.

Acts 5:3 "Then Peter said, 'Ananias, how is it that Satan has so filled your heart that you have lied to the Holy Spirit and have kept for yourself some of the money you received for the land?'"

Romans 16:20 "The God of peace will soon crush satan under your feet. The grace of our Lord Jesus be with you."

1 Corinthians 7:5 "Do not deprive each other except by mutual consent and for a time, so that you may devote yourselves to prayer. Then come together again so that satan will not tempt you because of your lack of self-control."

2 Corinthians 2:10,11 "I did it for your sakes in the presence of Christ, so that no advantage would be taken of us by satan, for we are not ignorant of his schemes."

2 Corinthians 11:3 "But I am afraid that, as the serpent deceived Eve by his craftiness, your minds will be led astray from the simplicity and purity of devotion to Christ."

2 Corinthians 11:14 "No wonder, for even satan disguises himself as an angel of light."

Ephesians 6:11 "Put on the full armor of God, so that you will be able to stand firm against the schemes of the devil."

2 Thessalonians 2:9 "The coming of the lawless one will be in accordance with the work of satan displayed in all kinds of counterfeit miracles, signs and wonders."

2 Thessalonians 3:3 "But the Lord is faithful, and He will strengthen and protect you from the evil one."

1 Timothy 3:7 "And he must have a good reputation with those outside the Church, so that he will not fall into reproach and the snare of the devil."

1 Timothy 5:14-15 "Therefore, I want younger widows to get married, bear children, keep house, and give the enemy no occasion for reproach; for some have already turned aside to follow satan."

2 Timothy 2:26 "And they may come to their senses and escape from the snare of the devil, having been held captive by him to do his will."

James 4:7 "Submit yourselves, then, to God. Resist the devil, and he will flee from you."

1 Peter 5:8 "Be self-controlled and alert. Your enemy the devil prowls around like a roaring lion looking for someone to devour."

1 John 2:13 "I am writing to you, fathers, because you know Him who has been from the beginning I am writing to you, young men, because you have overcome the evil one."

1 John 3:8 "He who does what is sinful is of the devil, because the devil has been sinning from the beginning. The reason the Son of God appeared was to destroy the devil's work."

1 John 5:18 "We know that no one who is born of God sins; but He who was born of God keeps him, and the evil one does not touch him."

Revelation 12:9 "And the great dragon was thrown down, the serpent of old who is called the devil and satan, who deceives the whole world; he was thrown down to the earth, and his angels were thrown down with him."

Revelation 20:1-2 "And I saw an angel coming down out of heaven, having the key to the Abyss and holding in his hand a great chain. He seized the dragon, that ancient serpent, who is the devil, or satan, and bound him for a thousand years."

Revelation 20:10 "And the devil, who deceived them, was thrown into the lake of burning sulfur, where the beast and the false prophet had been thrown. They will be tormented day and night for ever and ever."

Now, maybe it's just me, but I'm thinking that the Bible emphatically declares that a real live actual devil, satan, evil one, whatever you want to call him, actually exists, how about you? Old Testament, New Testament, from the beginning to the end, Genesis to Revelation, he's all over the place! And that's just thirty verses that's not all of them! Therefore, the point is this. How in the world can you sit there and say as a supposed Christian that he's just, "a mere symbol of evil?" It's crazy!

In fact, think about it, you have to deny what the Bible says in order to deny the existence of satan! Which last time I checked is not a good thing to do! In fact, it makes things even worse. Think about it. If I can't take these passages literally that speak of a literal devil, then why should I take anything else in the Bible literally? Maybe Jesus is not the only way to heaven, as the Bible literally says. Maybe God doesn't exist as the Bible literally says. Maybe God doesn't have a problem or punishment for sin! Maybe there is no hell, and nobody needs to be concerned about it at all whatsoever! And can I tell you something? That's precisely what the real devil wants people to believe. He's trying to send them to hell because that's where he too is headed to the Lake of Fire! That's how evil he is!

People, it is high time that we in the Church deal with the facts and acknowledge Biblical proof declaring that a literal satan does exists, in whom we literally have to deal with every single day. No wonder we're getting whooped on! There's a war going on and we're acting like it's a cakewalk and we need to know who our enemy is! He is not, "a mere symbol of evil." He is satan, the devil, the evil one and he does really exist!

The **second source** proving satan's existence is **The Societal Proof**.

Just look around. And this is a common-sense question but let me pose it anyway. "If satan is real, as the Bible clearly shows all over the place, Old and New Testament, and satan hasn't been destroyed yet, that happens at the end of the Millennium, he's probably still messing things up on planet earth today." How many of you can figure that out without any help? Well, guess what folks? That's exactly what we find all throughout our society when you look around. Satan is alive and well on planet earth unfortunately showing us he really does exist, even outside the Bible. In fact, what's ironic is the Bible says you can expect an increase of his activity on planet earth specifically in the last Days.

Revelation 9:20 "The rest of mankind that were not killed by these plagues still did not repent of the work of their hands; they did not stop worshiping demons, and idols of gold, silver, bronze, stone and wood – idols that cannot see or hear or walk."

But as you can see, as wild as it sounds, the Bible clearly says that in the Last Days, it's going to get so wicked that people are actually going to be worshipping demons, not God, demons, actual agents of evil! Not God! Can you believe that? But hey, good thing we don't see any signs of that happening in our society anytime soon huh? Yeah right folks, demon worship, including the worship of the biggest fallen angel himself, i.e. satan, is on the rise.

First of all, look around in our society, he's done a masterful job on us by getting us to act like him and live like him when we live for nothing but ourselves and love ourselves more than God...Which is the #1 law of satanism. Our whole world is acting like a bunch of devils! And two, it's gotten so bad, and so dark, that we now have full-blown satanists entering all levels of society. It's out in the open and it's on the rise. And part of the reason is due to our disbelief. We don't even think Satan exists, and so they sneak in under the radar with virtually no opposition. It's also partly because of satanism's ease of access. No longer do you have to go to some back alley in some creepy bookstore in Timbuktu to find out about satanism, it's all over the place, including the internet! And I quote, *"A surge in satanism is now being fueled by the internet and has led to a sharp rise in the demand for exorcisms"* ...you know...get these demons out of me!

There was even a prayer offered up by Jack Black to satan himself at an MTV video awards ceremony where he urged the audience to join hands and pray, *"Dear dark lord satan,"* and asked him, satan, to *"give the musicians and nominees continued success in the music industry."* Out in the open!

In fact, even some schools in California are saying, *"Lucifer is a model and a guardian." "Most of what contributes to our work as teachers – preparation work, artistic work, even meditative work, is under the guardianship of Lucifer. We can become great teachers under his supervision."*

It's now entering our school system period. *"A satanic temple has launched a campaign called "Protect Children Day" where they actually want children to pray openly to satan in school." "We want children to know that they are permitted to pray to satan in school."*

Yeah, you can't pray to God...but you can pray to satan in school. And even at the University level, they're starting to have satanic black masses. One was at Harvard, which believe it or not, was America's first school and it was started by a guy named Reverend John Harvard in 1636. And the schools' official motto used to be, "For Christ and the Church." ...not for satanism and the satanic temple!

And it's not stopping there! The rise of satanism and satan worship is now going full-blown into our Government. One man in Florida is right now seeking "equal time" in our Government to open up the meetings with a prayer to satan.... Is that going to help anything out? By the way, who is praying right now against President Trump? Witches. But hey, don't worry, that's all make believe. There's no spiritual war going on. They're just trying to get some press. Are you kidding me? And now statues of satan are getting ready to be put up at many of our government buildings, even in the Bible belt, as you can see below, *"For kids to look up to."*

We still don't think we are in a war? We still don't think that satan is real? Listen and look at the scripture. You cannot deny his existence without denying the scripture, which last time I checked is not a good thing to do. Look around, there is a massive surge of attention given to satan all over the place. And we still don't think satan is real? Folks look around! Satan and satanism is on the Rise just like the Bible said would happen in the Last Days. In fact, even the news is starting to blow the whistle on it:

"We believe in greed, we believe in selfishness." Says **Anton Szandor LaVey***, as he quotes from the Satanic Bible, "we believe in all the thoughts that motivate man because this is man's natural feelings."*

"This lady in a black robe came forward with this little baby," says the first woman. The second woman says, "I had my incredibly sharp knife". Then another declares, "I would strap the animal onto the middle of the pentagram." A second man says, "There were things that weren't quite as they should be." Lady #1 says, "And she just laid it on the alter." Then lady #2 says, "Then I just cut its head off, like that, suddenly," Lady #1 says, "Then the high priest just cut the baby's throat." A satanic priest tells that they taught him how to kill someone.

KPRC2 reports: *"There is a new tenant gaining a lot of attention north of Houston. The greater church of Lucifer is celebrating its grand opening later this month on Main Street and Keith Street in Old Town Spring."*

News 5 reports: *"Chaos and controversy has caused a slight delay at tonight's Pensacola council meeting. A leader from a Satanic Temple gave the invocation. The invocation started by David Sore, a representative of the Satanic Temple."*

Channel 7 reports: *"The largest public satanic ceremony in history is happening right here in Detroit. The lines ran around the graffiti wall with at least 100 people eagerly waiting for what has been kept well under wraps. It said dress like an animal or wear horns and tails", says one of the people in line. Some drove in from as far as upstate New York to see the satanic temple unveil a 9-foot-tall bronze statue of a goat headed satan. It seemed like an historic event", he said.*

Fox News reports: *"Group unveils plans for satan statue at Oklahoma Capitol. New York based satanic group wants to put a satan statue on the grounds of the Oklahoma state capitol and it has now unveiled drawings of its proposal so here it is. The statue features a bearded goat headed demon sitting on a throne with smiling kids next to it."*

Marina Portnaya says: *"This year a new book with games and lessons about satanism could be distributed to students attending public schools in Florida's Orange County. The ten-page satanic Children's Big Book of Activities features characters named Anabel and Damian who demonstrate rituals that explain Satanism."*

Fox 25 reports: *"It's called a Satanic Black Mass and it is about to happen at Harvard University. A Harvard University student club is hosting a satanic black mass reenactment to celebrate witchcraft and satanic worship."*

Fox news reports: *"A 17-year-old*

boy in Houston Texas will be charged as an adult for the rape and human sacrifice of a 15-year-old classmate of his who he killed in a satanic ritual, so he could sell his soul to the devil."

Where is the dividing line into full blown satanism? Worshipers are chanting "Hail satan, hail satan". "Something about sacrifice is that if you do it once you want to do it all the time." Says lady #2. LaVey says "All religions are coming around to satanism. We are in the very throws of a new satanic age. The evidence is all around us, all we have to do is look at it."[4]

But that's just it. We don't want to look at it. 91-99% close their eyes! But folks, it looks to me, according to the facts, that satan and satanism is on the rise in society, just like the Bible said would happen in the last days, and Revelation 9 said it would happen in the seven-year tribulation. Demon worship is all over the place. To me, on the one hand, it's kind of exciting, because if it is supposed to happen in the seven-year tribulation how much closer is the rapture? We don't know the date or the hour but that's getting close. These people aren't worshipping a figment of their imagination, "a mere symbol of evil," no they're worshipping a literal devil, a literal satan. And for those of you who still don't think this is a serious threat to our society, you need to deal with what these people do when they get together. It's sick, twisted, evil, and deadly. You don't want to be around when they do what they do, and you certainly don't want those satan worshippers to overtake your society. Let's take a look at their behavior:

WHY PEOPLE GET INTO SATANISM

- **It's Mysteriousness:** But they find out the hard way that it's a one-way ticket to a hell. One guy named Tony said, "I thought at first I could be a Satanist on just a philosophical level. But I could feel satan wanted me to go on to a higher level – to sacrificing bigger animals, then maybe to humans, then even to my life."

- **The Instability in Today's World:** Youth are looking for answers today in places where they normally wouldn't go.

- **Unusually Intense Pressures:** Stresses such as the breakup of the family unit, ever changing social customs, cries that the Church is irrelevant, and erosion of confidence in our Political system contribute to these pressures of daily life and many break under the load.

- **Extreme Loneliness:** The feeling that no one cares may lead people to become involved in the occult.

- **Mysticism:** The influence of Eastern religions in America and continued emphasis on psychic phenomena, mind-expanding drugs, have turned many to the mystical approach to life.

- **Music:** Glorifies satanism and Occult Themes.

- **Fantasy Role Playing Computer Games:** It's the "in thing" to do. Kids think it's neat and satanism is a way to amass power.

- **The Decline of the Family:** Traditional families of Dad, Mom, and a child or two is getting harder to find. Only 11% of all U.S. household fits this description. One satanist said, "If I had a close family relationship, I might not have gotten into satanism. There was an absence, and satan filled that."[5]

WHERE SATANISTS MEET

- Abandoned Churches (a favorite for obvious reasons)
- Cemeteries
- Mountainous Areas
- Desert Areas
- Beaches
- Abandoned Buildings
- Wooded Areas
- Basements
- Under Bridges
- Parks
- Business Locations After Hours[6]

WHEN DO SATANISTS MEET

- Jan 7 - St. Winebald Day (blood ritual - animal and/or human sacrifice and dismemberment - male, if human)

- Jan 17 - Satanic Revels (sexual ritual – Age 7-17 female)
- Jan 20-27 Abduction (Ceremonial preparation and holding of sacrificial victim for Candlemas - sexual and blood ritual - human sacrifice female or child any age)
- Jan 29 - St. Agnes Eve (Casting of spells)
- Feb. 2 – Candlemas (Sabbat or Witches Festival – blood ritual - animal and/or human sacrifice)
- Feb. 2 - Satanic Revels (sexual ritual – Age 7-17 female)
- Feb. 25 - St. Walpurgis Day (blood ritual - communion of blood and dismemberment - any age)
- Mar. 1 - St. Eichatadt (blood ritual - drinking of human blood for strength and homage to the demons - any age (male or female)
- Mar. 20 - date varies - Spring Equinox (Sabbat or Witches Festival – orgy ritual - any age (male or female, human or animal)
- Good Friday - Day of Passion - (mock the death of Christ – blood ritual - human sacrifice adult male only)
- Easter Eve Day – (blood ritual – human sacrifice – adult male or female)
- Apr 21-26 – Abduction (Ceremonial preparation and holding of sacrificial victim)
- Apr 26 - May 1 - Grand Climax – (sexual ritual – female – Age 1-25)

- June 21 - Coven Initiations – (First Day of Summer or Summer Solstice – orgy ritual - animal and/or human sacrifice - any age male or female or animal)
- Jul 1 - Demons Revel – (blood ritual - sexual association with demons - any age female)
- Jul 20-26 – Abduction (ceremonial preparation and holding of sacrificial victim for Grand Climax)

- Jul 27 - Grand Climax (5 weeks, 1 day after summer solstice - human sacrifice - female child or adult)
- Aug 1 - Lammas Day (Sabbat or Witches Festival – blood ritual - animal and/or human sacrifice - any age male or female)
- Aug 3 - Satanic Revels – (sexual ritual – Age 7-17 female)
- Aug 24 - St. Bartholomew's Day - (Great Sabbat and Fire festival)
- Sep 7 - Marriage to the Beast (sexual sacrifice and dismemberment - infant - 21 female)
- Sep 22 - date varies - Feast Day (Fall equinox – orgy ritual – any age)
- Oct 13-30 - Preparation for all Hallows Eve, Samhain (Halloween) - Abduction, holding and ceremonial preparation of individual for human sacrifice.
- Oct. 13 - Backward Halloween Date

- Oct 28-30 Satanist High Holy Day – (blood ritual - human sacrifice each day - any age male or female)
- Oct 30-31 - All Hallows Eve and Halloween – (Night of blood and sex for association with the demons - animal and/or human sacrifice - any age male or female and/or animal)
- Nov 1 - Satanist High Holy Day related to Halloween – (blood ritual - human sacrifice - any age male or female)
- Nov 4 - Satanic Revels – (sexual ritual – Age 7-17 female)
- Dec 22 - Winter Solstice (Sabbat or Witches Festival – orgy ritual - any age male or female, human or animal)

- Dec 24 – Demon Revels – (On Christmas Eve it is tradition for Satanists to give one another body parts from a Male infant.)[7]

WHAT DO SATANIC RITUALS LOOK LIKE

"As to why people get involved in these satanic rituals, many believe that human sacrifice will put a magic shield around them and their followers, protecting them from bullets or any other harm.

And the remains of their rituals are rather gruesome. Just one example is when authorities were searching for a missing college student and came to the end of their search when they found candles and kettles full of body parts, animal bones and a caldron containing brains, hearts, and other organs of victims. During the ritual killings, victim's brains were cut out and put on a fire, mixed with blood, herbs, rooster's feet, goat's heads, and turtles.

Officers found the bodies of thirteen males, one as young as fourteen. Several of the victims had been slashed with knives, others bludgeoned. One had been hanged, another apparently set afire, and at least two pumped with bullets. Some had been tortured with razor blades or had their hearts ripped out. Nearly all had been mutilated."[8]

And yet, nobody thinks this exists! What are we doing? Are we crazy? Not only the Bible, but even the evidence from Society is showing us unfortunately, that satan is alive and well on planet earth! He really exists! YET 91-99% says what we just saw is just a figment of your imagination! And yet, it's growing every single day! We don't even know who the enemy is! We don't even believe in him anymore! And yet, the whole time the Bible and Society is screaming to those who would deny satan's existence, "Are you nuts! Look around! Why do you think the world is falling apart? Proof of his existence is everywhere!"

And for those of you who are sufficiently freaked out at this point, and rightly so, because this is serious stuff…. this is serious evil…I want to share some good news. You see, the Bible says you don't have to be afraid of any of this activity if you're a Christian. Now, if you're not a Christian, you need to be very afraid because you're in a heap of trouble. You better get saved right now before it's too late for you because the enemy can mess with you until he's blue in the face! But if you are a Christian, remember these verses that God says about our condition in having to deal with satan:

1 John 4:4 "You are from God, little children, and have overcome them; because greater is He Who is in you than he who is in the world."

2 Timothy 1:7 "For God hath not given us the spirit of fear; but of power, and of love, and of a sound mind."

If you are a Christian you don't have to be afraid of the devil or satanists, or any of their activity. If you belong to Jesus, the devil can't touch you, without God's permission. But if you're not you better get saved right now. He is alive and well on planet earth. We're not on a cake walk we are in a war. This is serious. Again, if you're not saved you better be saved right now, the devil has already got you. There is no middle ground. Jesus said that you are either serving God or the entire time you think you are serving God in the middle ground and you're not a satinist, the devil had already got you. That's the lie. The only way you get out of the clutches of Satan and him having a hayday with you, is when you surrender to Jesus Christ and get set free. And when you become a Christian the devil can't touch you. Even this former devil worshipper found that out the hard way:

"It was all witches and warlocks, we lived on witchcraft, we had a contract direct with the devil himself. When I was younger, about 8 or 9 years old I would see my father go into his room to worship the devil and I could feel the presence of the devil come into that room and my father would worship and speak in tongues, demonic tongues, worship and put flowers and candles and water out at 7:00 o'clock at night to 5 in the morning. I was going to a demonic church. I was going to a witchcraft church. I was being trained to be a warlock. I was being trained with witches that were in the religion of 30, 40, 50 years. I was being trained to speak to principalities, spirits in the ground, the devil himself. You

couldn't speak to the devil right away, you had to earn your right to speak to the devil.

The first mass killing that they did in my neighborhood was right here. The husband stabbed her 52 times and cut her ears off. Then me and my brothers would hang out with her daughter and we came to the house with her daughter and she found her mother cut up into pieces.

At the age of 13, I was astral-projecting my body, I would leave my body at home and go to regents and curse the neighborhood, put the spirit of prostitution, spirit of drugs in the neighborhood, homosexuality here, spirit of demons here, spirit of murder here, spirit of suicide. I knew how to channel all the spirits into the neighborhood. At the age of 15, 16 years old I would go into hospitals and put the spirit of death in the ICU, spirit of death in all rooms. I wanted them to die because I wanted to be promoted to be the biggest devil worshiper in New York City.

I would move principalities from one region to another to control the demons on the ground, to cut down the church, cut down the growth of the church, to cut down the opportunity for people to get saved. If I told you I would kill you in 30 days, prepare yourself to die in 30 days. I don't care who you are, I don't care who you know, I don't care what religion you call yourself, a catholic or Christian, if you said you were a Christian, and you said you were a believer I was going to kill you, unless you had a real relationship with Jesus Christ.

I was involved in a conversation where someone was asked to kill a lady for $10,000. I said, 'I'll kill her', I said 'give me $7,000.00 and I'll kill her. I don't have to leave my house'. She said, 'by the way, she's a Christian'. I said, 'I'll kill her for free'. I said, 'I don't need the money. I'll kill her for free, I don't need the money, I'm going to teach these Christians a lesson. I don't want your money, I'll kill her for free'.

I did the voodoo thing, I did the witchcraft thing, twenty-one days went by and she didn't die. A month went by and she didn't die. I was like wow, what's going on. My reputation is on the line. I called the devil, I called demons, I increased the witchcraft, I doubled the witchcraft and so she could die overnight, nothing was going on, nothing was going on.

I was home at night and the devil showed up, the presence of the devil comes into my room and the devil told me we have to abort the plan for the lady you want to kill. I said I'm a witch, I'm a warlock, if I don't kill the lady they won't think I have any powers. He told me you don't understand, the God that she believes in says leave her alone. Don't touch her."9

      In other words, 1 John 4:4 "Greater is He Who is in me than he who is in this world." Even a former devil worshipper found that out the hard way. Folks, when are we going to wake up and realize that the Bible and even Society shows us, that contrary to the skeptical Church today, satan is real and he's alive and well on planet earth and we better take it seriously! We're not in a cakewalk Christian! We're in a war! This is not a game here on earth! This is a serious mission from God! And so, if you're reading this, and again, you're not saved, you need to realize that the devil's already got you and you're fair game. He can mess with you any way he wants! If that guy wanted to put a curse on you and kill you he could! You have no protection as a non-Christian. You better get saved now! and maybe that's why He's got you here today because God's trying to reach out and save you before it's too late!

      But if you are a Christian reading this, then it's time to get your head out of the sand! Its high time we stop being ignorant of the devil's schemes as Paul says! There's a war going on and it's not just abroad but its right here in our own country. It's a cosmic battle for the souls of men and women all around us. The stakes are high, and millions of lives are at risk. And if we're ever going to win this war then the American Church needs to once again shine for Jesus Christ and take this seriously! This is no time to be denying the existence of satan! We need to wake up Church! The alarm has sounded. We are under attack, it's *the Satanic War on the Christian*. Don't let the enemy get you! Amen?

Chapter Two

The Existence of Demons

"It happened in Pennsylvania over a three-day period and it involved the largest number of casualties in the entire war and became the largest battle ever in North America.

With its army in high spirits, the South intended to invade the North for a second time, but the North had other plans. Both armies collided in a single town and that's when the slaughter began.

Fierce fighting raged at Little Round Top, the Wheatfield, Devil's Den, and the Peach Orchard and more fighting commenced in the streets even at Cemetery Hill with full-scale assaults erupting across the battlefield. Yet, despite significant losses, the North held their lines.

Then on the third day of battle, the main event was a dramatic infantry assault led by 12,500 Southerners known as Pickett's Charge. But they were repulsed by the North, giving a historic loss to the Southern army. And when the dust cleared, and the smoke dissipated, and the firing stopped, 51,000 soldiers were killed, wounded, captured or missing.

The Battle not only became the turning point in the war and ended the South's attempt to ever invade the North again, but it even moved the President of the United States to make one of his most famous speeches ever, with words like this:

'Four score and seven years ago our fathers brought forth on this continent, a new nation, conceived in Liberty, and dedicated to the proposition that all men are created equal. We here highly resolve that these dead shall not have died in vain – that this nation, under God, shall have a new birth of freedom – and that government of the people, by the people, for the people, shall not perish from the earth.'

The war was the Civil War. The date was July 1-3, 1863. The Battle was Gettysburg."[1]

Now, how many of you have heard of the Battle of Gettysburg? I think we all have. And how many of you would say that battle was a horrific time for all those men and our nation's history. But with all due respect to those who lost their lives in the Battle of Gettysburg, if I were to tell you that I know of a battle that makes Gettysburg look like a time at the Grand Ole Opry? And what if I were to tell you that this battle didn't occur in just one place and one country at one time, but it's going on right now today all over the world and it's been leaving a trail of death and destruction for centuries. Folks, I'm talking once again about the *Satanic War on the Christian*. People, these are the facts. We Christians don't battle here and there once in a while, we go to war every single day. Whether you see it, feel it, believe it or not, the moment you got saved you entered into a spiritual war against a demonic host whose sole purpose is to destroy you and extinguish your effectiveness for Jesus Christ. And what's wild is that most wars go on for a few years or even longer. But *the Satanic War on the Christian* has been going on for the last 2,000 years, non-stop, and it's sending people straight into hell! And what's wild is most people will readily talk about all the other wars throughout history and all their atrocities, and rightly so…we have the History Channel…. we need to talk about them! YET how many people, even Christians, will openly discuss the longest war in mankind's history… The satanic War on the Christian that has destroyed more lives than all the wars put together? Therefore, in order to stop getting beat up as Christians, we're going to continue in our study, *the Satanic War on the Christian*. We saw last time that if you're ever going to win a war,

The first thing you must do is **Know Who Your Enemy is**…

It's common sense, right? And that enemy, that we have to deal with, is none other than the devil himself. He really does exist, contrary to popular opinion! But that is the problem. People today, even in the Church, don't even believe in a literal satan. We saw 91-99% say he's just a "figment of your imagination," i.e. "a mere symbol of evil." When the whole time, as we saw last time, the Biblical proof and the Societal proof is screaming out to us, "Are you nuts! Look around! Why do you think the world is falling apart? There is proof of his existence everywhere!" Open your eyes and get your head out of the sand! Deal with your enemy!
But that's not all. There is a second enemy we need to deal with. If we're going to stop getting beat up and duped all over the place as Christians in this satanic war it is the existence of demons. Folks, satan does not work alone. He's got a whole horde of evil hosts or demons that aid him in his evil attacks against us:

Mark 5:1-17 "They went across the lake to the region of the Gerasenes. When Jesus got out of the boat, a man with an evil spirit came from the tombs to meet Him. This man lived in the tombs, and no one could bind him anymore, not even with a chain. For he had often been chained hand and foot, but he tore the chains apart and broke the irons on his feet. No one was strong enough to subdue him. Night and day among the tombs and in the hills, he would cry out and cut himself with stones. When he saw Jesus from a distance, he ran and fell on his knees in front of Him. He shouted at the top of his voice, 'What do you want with me, Jesus, Son of the Most-High God? Swear to God that you won't torture me!' For Jesus had said to him, 'Come out of this man, you evil spirit!' Then

Jesus asked him, 'What is your name?' 'My name is Legion,' he replied, 'for we are many.' And he begged Jesus again and again not to send them out of the area. A large herd of pigs was feeding on the nearby hillside. The demons begged Jesus, 'Send us among the pigs; allow us to go into them.' He gave them permission, and the evil spirits came out and went into the pigs. The herd, about two thousand in number, rushed down the steep bank into the lake and were drowned. Those tending the pigs ran off and reported this in the town and countryside, and the people went out to see what had happened. When they came to Jesus, they saw the man who had been possessed by the legion of demons, sitting there, dressed and in his right mind; and they were afraid. Those who had seen it told the people what had happened to the demon-possessed man – and told about the pigs as well. Then the people began to plead with Jesus to leave their region."

In other words, they were more concerned about the pigs, their livelihood, than a human being set free from demons. Sounds like today, doesn't it? But folks, according to our text, I'm kind of thinking that demons and evil spirits really do exist, and they really do possess people! Anybody else coming to the same conclusion? Yeah hello, they're not only mentioned once, not twice, but 8 times in just this one passage from Jesus! Three as evil spirits, three as demons, and two as a Legion, or Legion of demons. And by the way, a Roman Legion back in the day was upwards to 5,000 or more men! So, this guy had a ton of demons in him! In fact, each pig that went off the bank and died probably had more than one in them![2]

But this is the problem! The Bible is clear, yet the Church today is losing *the Satanic War on the Christian* because they don't even know who this second enemy is! And they don't know who it is because they're denying its existence too! They not only deny the existence of satan, but they also deny the existence of his evil cohorts, the demons, as well, even though the Bible is extremely emphatic about it!! And part of the problem is the media, always downplaying it, acting like it's a big joke, when it's not, like these commercials reveal:

As a man is walking his dog down a deserted road after dark they are passing by this big beautiful three-story house on the corner. It looks normal with kids toys in the front yard, but then suddenly the man and dog stop when they realize that all the lights in the house are flickering on and off. He stops dead in his tracks and stares at the house. "What's happening?" he asks his dog. This house must be haunted.

The next scene is a little boy in a restaurant playing with his dads' cell phone. Pushing all the buttons. The mother grabs the phone and sees that her son was turning the lights on and off at home. She turns to her husband and says, "Your son is playing with the lights again."

The speaker for the commercial comes on and proceeds to tell the audience that in the modern world you can control just about anything with an app. With the Esurance mobile app., you can do the same thing with your car insurance, like access your ID card, file a claim, or manage your policy, it's so easy its almost scary.

Then, once again you see the man walking his dog. He picks up his little dog and runs to get away from the haunted house.

The next commercial is of another big house with the lights flashing. A priest is standing outside looking at it wondering what is going on. He decides to go inside to see what is causing such a commotion. He looks in one of the rooms and there he finds an old man with his head bowed and his hands clasped together praying.

He proceeds to go upstairs and as he reaches the top of the stairs he hears a woman screaming. He hesitated a minute, but the screaming doesn't stop. He walks a little closer to the door where the screaming is coming from. As he walks on the floor it creaks with each step. He kisses his crucifix and begins to turn the door knob.

He slowly opens the door, looks around the room, and then she screams one more time, this time he sees her stuck to the ceiling, screaming and throwing her arms and legs around. On the table is a Bible with blowing pages. He immediately

backs up, in shock of what he sees going on in this room. A woman is being dragged around the ceiling, screaming for help.

But as the camera pans away to show the upper floor you see a little old woman vacuuming her floor. As she vacuums, she is singing and dancing and unable to hear the lady downstairs. The suction from the vacuum is so great that it has caught the lady downstairs by surprise and is holding her tightly to the ceiling.

She can't get away no matter how much she screams and pushes to be released. The commercial ends with 'You know when it's the devil, Dirt Devil.[3]

Yeah, that's all it was, it was a kid messing with the lights from a cell phone. No, no. It was just a super strong vacuum cleaner on the second floor, that's all it was, this freaky activity going on and on and on and on it goes. But seriously folks, this is what the media does. They downplay this topic, not just satan, but demons and demon possession. They act like it's no big deal when it IS! They are just as evil and just as real as satan…they too really exist!

The **first and primary source** proving the existence of demons is **the Biblical Proof**.

Believe it or not, Mark 5 is just one of many passages in the Bible showing and proving the existence of literal demons, over and over again, and whom we really have to deal with. There really is a war going on! Old Testament, New Testament, they are mentioned all over the place. So, let's take a look at some of that proof:

Deuteronomy 32:17 "They sacrificed to demons, which are not God – gods they had not known, gods that recently appeared, gods your fathers did not fear."

Psalm 106:37-39 "They sacrificed their sons and their daughters to demons. They shed innocent blood, the blood of their sons and daughters, whom they sacrificed to the idols of Canaan, and the land was desecrated by their blood. They defiled themselves by what they did; by their deeds they prostituted themselves."

Leviticus 17:7 "They shall no longer sacrifice their sacrifices to the goat demons with which they play the harlot."

Isaiah 13:21 "But desert beasts will lie down there, and their houses will be full of howling creatures; there owls will dwell, and goat-demons will dance there."

2 Chronicles 11:15 "Jeroboam appointed his own priests for the high places, the goat-demons, and the golden calves he had made."

Matthew 4:24 "News about Him spread all over Syria, and people brought to Him all who were ill with various diseases, those suffering severe pain, the demon-possessed, those having seizures, and the paralyzed, and He healed them."

Matthew 8:16 "When evening came, many who were demon-possessed were brought to Him, and He drove out the spirits with a word and healed all the sick."

Matthew 8:28 "When He arrived at the other side in the region of the Gadarenes, two demon-possessed men coming from the tombs met Him. They were so violent that no one could pass that way."

Matthew 9:32 "While they were going out, a man who was demon-possessed and could not talk was brought to Jesus."

Matthew 12:22 "Then they brought Him a demon-possessed man who was blind and mute, and Jesus healed him, so that he could both talk and see."

Matthew 15:22 "A Canaanite woman from that vicinity came to Him, crying out, 'Lord, Son of David, have mercy on me! My daughter is suffering terribly from demon-possession.'"

Matthew 17:18 "Jesus rebuked the demon, and it came out of the boy, and he was healed from that moment."

Mark 1:32 "That evening after sunset the people brought to Jesus all the sick and demon-possessed."

Mark 7:26 "The woman was a Greek, born in Syrian Phoenicia. She begged Jesus to drive the demon out of her daughter."

Luke 4:33-35 "In the synagogue there was a man possessed by a demon, an evil spirit. He cried out at the top of his voice, 'What do you want with us, Jesus of Nazareth? Have you come to destroy us? I know Who You are – the Holy One of God!' 'Be quiet!' Jesus said sternly. 'Come out of him!' Then the demon threw the man down before them all and came out without injuring him."

Luke 8:27,29 "When Jesus stepped ashore, he was met by a demon-possessed man from the town. For a long time, this man had not worn clothes or lived in a house but had lived in the tombs. For Jesus had commanded the evil spirit to come out of the man. Many times, it had seized him, and though he was chained hand and foot and kept under guard, he had broken his chains and had been driven by the demon into solitary places."

Luke 8:36 "Those who had seen it told the people how the demon-possessed man had been cured."

Luke 9:42 "Even while the boy was coming, the demon threw him to the ground in a convulsion. But Jesus rebuked the evil spirit, healed the boy and gave him back to his father."

Luke 11:14 "Jesus was driving out a demon that was mute. When the demon left, the man who had been mute spoke, and the crowd was amazed."

John 7:20 "'You are demon-possessed,' the crowd answered. 'Who is trying to kill you?'"

John 8:48-49 "The Jews answered him, 'Aren't we right in saying that you are a Samaritan and demon-possessed?' 'I am not possessed by a demon,' said Jesus, 'but I honor my Father and you dishonor Me."

John 8:52 "At this the Jews exclaimed, 'Now we know that you are demon-possessed!'"

John 10:20-21 "Many of them said, 'He is demon-possessed and raving mad. Why listen to Him?' But others said, 'These are not the sayings of a man possessed by a demon. Can a demon open the eyes of the blind?'"

Acts 19:13-16 "Some Jews who went around driving out evil spirits tried to invoke the name of the Lord Jesus over those who were demon-possessed. They would say, 'In the name of the Jesus whom Paul preaches, I command you to come out.' Seven sons of Sceva, a Jewish chief priest, were doing this. One day the evil spirit answered them, 'Jesus I know, and Paul I know about, but who are you?' Then the man who had the evil spirit jumped on them and overpowered them all. He gave them such a beating that they ran out of the house naked and bleeding."

1 Corinthians 10:20-21 "The sacrifices of pagans are offered to demons, not to God, and I do not want you to be participants with demons. You cannot drink the cup of the Lord and the cup of demons too; you cannot have a part in both the Lord's table and the table of demons."

1 Timothy 4:1 "The Spirit clearly says that in later times some will abandon the faith and follow deceiving spirits and things taught by demons."

James 2:19 "You believe that there is one God. Good! Even the demons believe that – and shudder."

Revelation 9:20 "The rest of mankind that were not killed by these plagues still did not repent of the work of their hands; they did not stop worshiping demons, and idols of gold, silver, bronze, stone and wood – idols that cannot see or hear or walk."

Revelation 16:14 "For they are spirits of demons, performing signs, which go out to the kings of the whole world, to gather them together for the war of the great day of God, the Almighty."

Revelation 18:2 "And he cried out with a mighty voice, saying, 'Fallen, fallen is Babylon the great! She has become a dwelling place of demons and a prison of every unclean spirit, and a prison of every unclean and hateful bird.'"

Maybe it's just me, but I'm kind of thinking that the Bible emphatically declares that real live demons actually exist, how about you? Old Testament, New Testament, from the beginning to the end, they're all over the place! And that's just thirty verses, that's not all of them! In fact, the Bible even specifically says that "Jesus came to set the captives free," and in the context of that statement, He's not talking about those "in a poor economic situation" and a "low self-esteem." Rather it has to deal with the compassion of setting people free from demonic possession as we just read. That's why He's casting out so many demons…He's doing what He said the Messiah would do, He's setting the captives free!

But my point is this. How in the world can you sit there and say as a supposed Christian that demons are not real…that "It's a figment of your imagination?" "It's a scare tactic from Preachers to get your money." …. When they're mentioned all over the place! It's crazy! And again, just like with satan, you can't deny the existence of demons without denying the teaching of the

Bible. Which last time I checked is not a good thing to do! If I can't take these passages literally that speak of literal demons, Old Testament, New Testament, then why should I take anything else in the Bible literally? Maybe Jesus is not the Messiah, who's come to set the captives free, as the Bible literally says. Maybe demons don't really possess people. Maybe there is another way to Heaven. Maybe the One World Religion Harlot has it right after all. Maybe we really could take on God and defeat Him at the Battle of Armageddon! Are you kidding me? That's precisely what the real demons want people to believe. They're trying to send them to hell because that's where they too are headed, the Lake of Fire! That's how evil they are!

And so, to me, that's the ultimate obvious question. They obviously exist, demons, we just saw that in the Bible. "But where did they come from? Why are they here and what are they up to?" right? Anybody else wondering that? Well, let's look at the evidence:

THE ORIGIN OF DEMONS

Angels
(Hebrew – Malak – Messenger)
(Greek – Angelos – Messenger)

Holy/Unfallen/Elect	Unholy/Fallen/Demon
1 Timothy 5:21	Satan – Isaiah 14:12-15
	Demons – Rev. 12

1 Timothy 5:21 "I charge you, in the sight of God and Christ Jesus and the elect angels, to keep these instructions without partiality, and to do nothing out of favoritism."

Isaiah 14:12-15 "How you have fallen from heaven, O morning star, son of the dawn! You have been cast down to the earth, you who once laid low the nations! You said in your heart, 'I will ascend to heaven; I will raise my throne above the stars of God; I will sit enthroned on the mount of assembly, on the utmost heights of the sacred mountain. I will ascend above the tops of the clouds; I will make myself like the Most-High.' But you are brought down to the grave, to the depths of the pit."

Revelation 12:4 "His tail swept a third of the stars out of the sky and flung them to the earth."[4]

THE LOCATION OF DEMONS

Demons

Bound or Confined	Active
	Ephesians 6/ Today
Tartarus (Permanent)	Future/Torment
2 Peter 2:4/Jude 6	Matthew 25
Pit (Temporary)	
Revelation 9:2,3,10,15	

Ephesians 6:12,13 "For our struggle is not against flesh and blood, but against the rulers, against the authorities, against the powers of this dark world and against the spiritual forces of evil in the heavenly realms. Therefore, put on the full armor of God, so that when the day of evil comes, you may be able to stand your ground."

2 Peter 2:4 "For if God did not spare angels when they sinned, but sent them to hell, (Tartarus) putting them into gloomy dungeons to be held for judgment."

Jude 6 "And the angels who did not keep their positions of authority but abandoned their own home – these He has kept in darkness, bound with everlasting chains for judgment on the great Day."

Revelation 9:2,3,10,15 "When he opened the Abyss, smoke rose from it like the smoke from a gigantic furnace. And out of the smoke locusts came down upon the earth. They had tails and stings like scorpions, and in their tails, they had power to torment people for five months. And the four angels who had been kept ready for this very hour and day and month and year were released to kill a third of mankind."

Matthew 25:41 "Then He will say to those on His left, 'Depart from Me, you who are cursed, into the eternal fire prepared for the devil and his angels.'"[5]

THE IDENTITY OF DEMONS

Demons are not Dead People: Some people would have you and I believe that demons are simply the spirits of dead people who were really wicked. However, we know this can't be true Bible declares that when people die, they go to one of two places, heaven or hell and when you get there you don't come back. For the saved, they go straight into heaven (2 Corinthians 5:8 "Absent from the body is to be present with the Lord.") and for the unsaved, they go to straight into hell (Luke 16:22,23 "The rich man also died and was buried. In hell, where he was in torment.")

Both are places of no return (Job 7:9-10 "As a cloud vanishes and is gone, so he who goes down to the grave does not return. He will never come to his house again; his place will know him no more." Luke 16:26 "And besides all this, between us and you a great chasm has been fixed, so that those who want to go from here to you cannot, nor can anyone cross over from there to us."

So those in heaven remain in heaven and those in hell remain in hell until the end of the Millennial Kingdom where those in hell will be brought up from hell to be judged before God (Revelation 20:12 "And I saw the dead, great and small, standing before the throne, and books were opened.") and then they will be cast into the Lake of Fire. (Revelation 20:14 "Then death and Hades were thrown into the lake of fire. The lake of fire is the second death.")

Also, if one does see a "spirit entity" claiming to be a deceased "loved one" or some other "historical figure" it is an actual demon "impersonating" that person who is in heaven or hell and the Bible calls these demons "familiar spirits" those who would seek to deceive people and lead them away from God by appearing as a dead person." (Leviticus 19:31 "Do not turn to spirits of the dead, and do not inquire of familiar spirits, to be defiled by them. I am the LORD your God.")

Demons are not a Pre-Adamic Race of People: Some people would actually believe that there was a whole race of people who existed prior to Adam and they are the ones we should identity as the demons.

This false belief is arrived from another false teaching called "The Gap Theory" that presupposes that there was a "gap" between Genesis 1:1 and Genesis 1:2 and that in this "gap" there was a whole race of people who existed but perished millions of years ago.

Part of the reason this was "invented" was to try to "help" explain the lie of Evolution's claim that we have been here for millions and billions of years instead of roughly 6,000 years as the Bible clearly teaches.

First, evolution is a lie and I don't need to defend a lie. Secondly, there is no Scriptural support whatsoever for this view. The Bible declares that Adam was the first man (1 Corinthians 15:45 "So it is written: 'The first man Adam became a living being.'") and that there was no death prior to Adam (Romans 5:12,14 "Therefore, just as sin entered the world through one man, and death through sin, and in this way, death came to all men…death reigned from the time of Adam.")

There was no race of people prior to Adam therefore they cannot be identified as the demons.

Demons are not a Hybrid Version of People: This is the false belief that demons are the "Nephilim" mentioned in the Bible that arose from the mingling of fallen angels and the daughters of men as mentioned in the Genesis 6 account. (Genesis 6:4 "The Nephilim were on the earth in those days – and also afterward – when the sons of God went to the daughters of men and had children by them. They were the heroes of old, men of renown.")

Thus, they say these "Nephilim" created by this fallen angel/human hybrid going on and that were destroyed by the flood became the demons that we must deal with today. However, this view, like the previous two, is without the slightest Biblical evidence whatsoever.

Rather people try to justify this false belief by using an albeit popular, yet non-Biblical book called The Book of Enoch. It is an interesting historical book, but it is not the inspired, inerrant, and authoritative Word of God. It didn't make the canon for good reason and thus we should never base a belief exclusively, or even primarily, on extra-biblical literature and yet this is what these people are doing.

Rather, many Biblical scholars believe that the "Nephilim" were real and perished in the flood along with the rest of the wicked souls on earth, save Noah & his family, but they went to hell, they did not become the demons. In fact, Biblically, it is these "fallen angels" (demons) who did this ungodly act of mingling with the daughters of men to create these "Nephilim" who are the ones the Bible says are "confined" or "imprisoned" because of this very act.

2 Peter 2:4 "For if God did not spare angels when they sinned, but sent them to hell, (Tartarus) putting them into gloomy dungeons to be held for judgment."

Jude 6 "And the angels who did not keep their positions of authority but abandoned their own home – these He has kept in darkness, bound with everlasting chains for judgment on the great Day."

Jude 7 "Even as Sodom and Gomorra, and the cities about them in like manner, giving themselves over to fornication, and going after strange flesh, are set forth for an example, suffering the vengeance of eternal fire."

Thus, this explains why these demons are not allowed to roam the earth like the other demons today as we saw on the chart and are thus confined. They went after "strange flesh" the daughters of men and God has imprisoned them for it.

Demons are Fallen Angels: The most logical Biblical conclusion is that the word demon is simply another title or name for fallen angels and that's why most conservative Biblical scholars believe that demons are simply fallen or evil angels, cohorts of satan, the third of the angelic host who rebelled with him.[6]

So that's who they are. But folks, here's my point. How much more proof do we need before we deal with the facts and the Biblical proof declaring that literal demons exist in whom we literally must deal with every single day. No wonder we're getting whooped on! There's a war going on and we're acting like it's a cakewalk and we need to know who our enemy is! Demons are not, "a figment of our imagination" and they're not "A "scare tactic from Preachers to get your money!" They really exist, just like satan, they really are real, and they're really out to get you! We need to deal with it, not deny it!

The **second source** proving the existence of demons is **The Societal Proof**.

And once again this is a common-sense question but let me pose it anyway. "If demons are real, as the Bible clearly shows all over the place, Old and New Testament, and some demons are still able to roam around and mess with people, then they're probably still messing things up on planet earth today." How many of you can figure that out without any help? Well guess what folks? That's exactly what we find all throughout our society when you look around. Demons are active in all four corners of the planet showing us they really do exist, even outside the Bible. In fact, you go to any Third World country and there seems to be an abundance of them:

"In Europe, I know that people don't believe that there are demons or evil spirits" one man says. "Are you bad, I want to know, In the mighty name of Jesus I command you to come out, what is your name? Demon I command you now, what is your name?" The priest is holding down the possessed man while trying to deliver him of the demon. The man is groaning and trying to get away, but he is being firmly held down. "What is your name, what is your name?"

Then we go to another part of Africa where there is a woman that is possessed by a demon. They are dancing to get ready for her to perform. "They called me and when I saw her it became clear to me that she had a spirit in her." A woman at the ceremony says. "It is a cobra. Now I will make an oracle out of her, so that the spirit can talk through her. She has to be taken through the ritual." Says the priest. To get her ready they pour blood over her body, and she is in a trance being controlled by the demon of the cobra. She is now a cobra with her tongue going in and out like a snake.

A Christian minister that is working with the people of Ghana is telling that this is a practice rooted in the satanic kingdom not in the kingdom of God. And everything that is of Satan is evil and demonic and we can't accept those things."

He then places his hand on her head and says, "I set you free in Jesus name."[7]

Setting the captives free still to this day, just like Jesus did, and what Paul did in the Book of Acts. He too had to deal with a snake spirit. Were you paying attention there? That guy said it was a Cobra.

Acts 16:16 "Now it happened of us going to the place of prayer, a certain girl, having a spirit of Python, met us, who was bringing her masters much gain by fortune-telling."

And Paul cast it out and the people got upset with him…just like today. But here's the point. If you look around, especially in Third World countries, demons are all over the place just like in the Bible. The locals don't doubt it. They deal with it every day! And yet, that's the problem. We here in the West act like it doesn't happen here, when it does. In fact, I think it might be happening on a grander scale but we're oblivious to it because of the lie of Secular Psychology. They have trained us to think that people who are demon possessed, like that girl, aren't really possessed. No! No! No! They say, "These people have some form of psychological aberration and we just need to drug them into oblivion and keep them quiet." …as if that helps. They basically say, "We're too sophisticated for that kind of irrational thinking."

Now, I've been to many a Psych Ward in twenty years plus of ministry, and I will tell you first hand that not all those people are suffering from something just physical or mental. Something spiritual is going on. Two, the irony is when you look at the Founders of Secular Psychology they too were involved in demonic practices and pushed demonic drugs to get people in an altered state of consciousness to connect with demons making things even worse! And Lord willing, we'll get to that in the next study. But all you have to do, folks, is look around. We live in a society today full of people who are full-blown demon possessed just like third world countries. It's not a "psychological aberration. It's happening here. It's just we don't want to believe it, because we've been trained by False teachers to turn a blind eye to it. But the examples are everywhere. I only have time to share two. One from a man, one from a woman"

"A man reaches into the refrigerator at a grocery store and pulls out a bottle of cold water but as he goes to close the door he seems to be having a seizure standing in the aisle. The other patrons stop what they are doing to see if this man is all right. He drops the water on the floor and starts saying things that is not comprehendible to the human ear. While making these noises he stands shaking and resembles a seizure. He pulls at his clothing and then falls to the floor. Again, a patron looks at him wondering if she should help him, but he points his finger at her and yells. She immediately turns and runs.

Another case is where a woman is sitting in alley grabbing at her throat, groaning with convulsions. But this time she is also spitting out blood as she groans. It seems she has bitten off her tongue. She gets up and runs down the alley screaming, bleeding, and convulsing all at the same time.[8]

But don't worry. That was just a vacuum cleaner. Somebody's messing around with their cell phone. Folks, it looks to me like, demons and demon possession is all over the place, even here in America, how about you? Yet many of us have been wrongly trained by the God-hating teachings of Secular Psychology to turn a blind eye and the captives are not being set free. Not only the Bible, but even the evidence from Society is showing us that demons are alive and well on planet earth. They really exist! They're not just a "psychological aberration!"

And for those of you who are sufficiently freaked out at this point, and rightly so, because this is serious stuff…. this is serious evil…I want to share some good news. You see, the Bible says if you're a Christian, you don't have to be afraid of any of this activity. Now, if you're not a Christian, you need to be very afraid because you're in a heap of trouble. You better get saved right now before it's too late because the enemy can mess with you anyway he wants and possess you all he wants! But if you are a Christian, remember these verses that God says about our condition in having to deal with not just satan, but now demons:

1 Corinthians 3:16 "Don't you know that you yourselves are God's temple and that God's Spirit lives in you?"

John 14:23 "Jesus replied, "If anyone loves Me, he will obey My teaching. My Father will love him. We will come to him & make Our home with him.

In other words, if God the Spirit, and God the Father, and God the Son has made their home in me as a Christian and I have become Their temple then there's no way in the world I can even become demon-possessed again! I can be externally oppressed as a Christian, but I can never be possessed because God isn't going to scooch over in His Temple and make room for a demon!

But I'll say it again, if you're reading this and you're not a Christian you can be oppressed and possessed all at the same time because you don't belong to God and you're not His temple! You better get saved now!

Christian, it is high time we get your head out of the sand and stop being ignorant of the devil's schemes! And stop listening to Secular Psychology!

There's a war going on and it's not just abroad, its right here in our own country. It's a cosmic battle for the souls of men and women all around us. The stakes are high, and millions of lives are at risk. And if we're ever going to win this war then the American Church needs to once again shine for Jesus Christ and take this seriously! This is no time to be denying the existence of demons! We need to wake up Church! The alarm has sounded. We are under attack, it's *the Satanic War on the Christian.* Don't let the enemy get you! Amen?

Chapter Three

The Character of Satan

"It was the last major German offensive of WWII and the largest and bloodiest battle fought by the United States in all that War.

The Germans attempted to push the Allied forces back from German territory, with 450,000 German troops along with 1,500 tanks, tank destroyers, assault guns, and over 4,000 artillery pieces. And at first, the Germans were overwhelmingly successful.

But the combined forces of the six Allied Armies began to take its toll. General Dwight Eisenhower had at his disposal 48 divisions distributed over a 600-mile front and General George S. Patton successfully maneuvered the Third Army to neutralize the German counteroffensive.

Then to make matters worse, the Germans ran out of fuel and the military losses began to mount. And that's when Adolf Hitler ordered all able-bodied men between the ages of 16 and 60 to defend their homeland. But the damage was already done. The German Airforce had been totally shattered, their last reserves were now gone, the Germans were forced to retreat, and face the inevitable. The Allies were taking over Germany.

When the smoke had cleared, and the bombs had stopped, the Allies lost nearly 100,000 men and the Germans 125,000 men. It was the costliest action ever fought by the U.S. Army alone.

The date was December 16, 1944–January 16, 1945. The Battle was The Battle of the Bulge."[1]

Now folks, how many of you have heard of the Battle of The Bulge? I think most of us have. And how many of you would say that battle was a terrible time for all the men there? But with all due respect to those who gave their lives in the Battle of the Bulge, what if I were to tell you that I know of a battle that makes The Battle of the Bulge look like a backyard scuffle? What if I were to tell you that this battle didn't occur in just one place and one country at one time, but it's going on right now today all over the world and it's been leaving a trail of death and destruction for centuries. Folks, I'm talking once again about *the Satanic War on the Christian.*
And these are the facts. We Christians don't battle here and there once in a while. We go to war, every single day. Whether you see it, feel it, believe it or not, the moment you were saved you entered a spiritual war against a demonic host whose sole purpose is to destroy you and extinguish your effectiveness for Jesus Christ. What's wild, is that most wars go on for a few years or even longer. But *the Satanic War on the Christian* has been going on for the last 2,000 years non-stop and it's sending people straight into hell! Most people will readily talk about all the other wars throughout history and all their atrocities, and rightly so…we have the History Channel. We need to talk about them! How many people, even Christians, will openly discuss the longest war in mankind's history…*the Satanic War on the Christian* that has destroyed more lives than all the wars put together? Therefore, in order to stop getting duped and beat up all over the place, we're going to continue in our study, *the Satanic War on the Christian.*

The last two times we saw that if you're ever going to win a war, then the **first thing** you must do is **Know Who Your Enemy Is,** amen?

It's common sense, right? And so far, we've seen that enemy is none other than Satan and last time we saw it was ALSO the demons as well. They really do exist, contrary to the LIE of Secular Psychology! But that was the problem. We have been brainwashed by these False Teachers, even in the Church, to not believe in literal demons, instead fall for the lie that we're much more sophisticated than that. Don't you realize that "It's just a figment of your imagination" or a "Vacuum Cleaner" or a "Scare tactic from Preachers to get your money" or it's somebody "messing with their cell phone" when the whole time, the Biblical proof and the Societal proof screaming out to us, "Are you nuts! Look around! Why do you think the world is so messed up? Proof of their existence is everywhere!" Open your eyes, get your head out of the sand, and deal with our enemy! But that's not all.

The second thing we need to deal with if we're going to stop getting beat up and duped all over the place as Christians in this *Satanic War on the Christian* is **The Character of Our Enemy.**

That's right folks, you not only need to know who your enemy is, but you also need to know what they're like. What their character is like. And folks, the character of satan is not good. He is evil, rotten, deceptive to the core! You don't want to mess with him!

Revelation 12:1-9 "A great and wondrous sign appeared in heaven: a woman clothed with the sun, with the moon under her feet and a crown of twelve stars on her head. She was pregnant and cried out in pain as she was about to give birth. Then another sign appeared in heaven: an enormous red dragon with seven heads and ten horns and seven crowns on his heads. His tail swept a third of the stars out of the sky and flung them to the earth. The dragon stood in front of the woman who was about to give birth, so that he might devour her child the moment it was born. She gave birth to a son, a male child, who will rule all the nations with an iron scepter. And her child was snatched up to God and to his throne. The woman fled into the desert to a place prepared for her by God, where she might be taken care of for 1,260 days. And there was war in heaven. Michael and his angels fought against the dragon, and the dragon and his angels fought back. But he was not strong enough, and they lost their place in heaven. The great dragon was hurled down – that ancient serpent called the devil, or Satan, who leads the whole world astray. He was hurled to the earth, and his angels with him."

In other words, he lost! He's the big loser, not us! But folks, according to our text, I'm kind of thinking that satan's character is something you don't want to mess with, it's pretty rotten! Anybody else coming to the same conclusion? He's not only called, in this one passage alone, a great dragon, an ancient serpent, the devil, satan, and the one who leads the whole world astray, but he wanted to even kill Jesus, the Messiah, and annihilate Israel!

But here is the problem! People, even in the Church, are not only denying his existence today, including the demons, the third that fell with him here in this passage, but because of that, they never get around to understanding his character. They don't believe in him, so they don't know what they're up against! And if you're ever going to win a war you got to know what you're up against, right? What is the Character of your Enemy! What are they like? What are they up to? It's common sense, right? So that's what we're going to do. We're going to look now at the Character of satan, so we don't get blindsided by his attacks, amen?

The first and primary source showing us the character of satan is **The Biblical Proof.**

Believe it or not folks, Revelation 12 is just one of many passages in the Bible that reveals to us the character of satan, over and over again, with whom we really have to deal with. There really is a war going on! Old Testament, New Testament, his character is mentioned all over the place, so we don't get caught off guard. He is flat out evil! Let's take a look at some of that proof:

THE CHARACTER OF SATAN

- Accuser – Opposes Believers Before God – Revelation 12:10
- Adversary – A Rival Opponent in a Conflict – Job 1
- Angel of Light – Appears as Good When Really Evil – 2 Corinthians 11:14
- Beelzebub – Lord of the Flies/Dung – Matthew 12:24
- Belial – Worthless – 2 Corinthians 6:15
- Deceiver – Leads People Away from Truth & into Error – Revelation 12:9
- Devil – One Who Slanders/Falsely Accuses – Matthew 4:1
- Enemy – Hostile Opponent – Matthew 13:28/1 Peter 5:8
- Evil One – Intrinsically Evil (poneros) – John 17:15
- God of the World – Controls Philosophy of this World – 2 Corinthians 4:4
- Great Red Dragon – Destructive Creature – Revelation 12:3,7,9
- Liar – Perverts the Truth – John 8:44
- Murderer – Leads People to Physical & Eternal Death – John 8:44

- Power of this Dark World – Creator of Dark Activity – Ephesians 6:12
- Prince of Devils – Commander of Demons – Matthew 12:24
- Prince of the Power of the Air – Ruler of Demonic Realm – Ephesians 2:2
- Prince of this World – Authority Behind Our Wicked World – John 12:31
- Roaring Lion – Vicious Animal Seeking to Devour People – 1 Peter 5:8
- Ruler of this World – The Chief Leader Behind World System – John 12:31
- Satan – Incites People to Sin & Turn Away from God – Matthew 4:10
- Serpent – Crafty deceiver – Genesis 3:4/2 Corinthians 11:3
- Serpent of Old – The Original Deceiver in Eden – Revelation 12:9
- Spirit of Those Who are Disobedient – Gets People to Oppose God's Will – Ephesians 2:2
- Tempter – One Who Solicits People to Sin – Matthew 4:3
- Wicked One – Evil Corrupt & Morally Wrong – Matthew 13:19[2]

Maybe it's just me, but I'm kind of thinking that the Bible emphatically declares that a real live actual wicked entity called satan, the devil, the wicked one, really does exist. His character is evil and rotten to the core, right? He is not a nice guy! Nothing to mess with! And that's just twenty-five descriptions of his character, that's not all of them! Old Testament, New Testament, from the beginning to the end, his character is revealed to us over and over again, so we don't get caught off guard! This guy is real and he's really evil and rotten to the core! God wants us to know his character, so we're not caught off guard, we know what we're up against, so we don't get blindsided!

And so, this is the point. How in the world can you sit there and say, as a supposed Christian, that satan's not real, no big deal, nothing to worry about, he's just "a figment of your imagination," "a mere symbol of evil" when God tells us so much about him and how evil he really is for our own good! It's crazy! No wonder we're getting whooped on! We not only don't know who our enemy is, because we refuse to believe in him, but we don't even know what we're up against, because nobody wants to deal with his evil character. We need to get our head out of the sand and deal with reality! It is high time that we, in the Church, deal with the facts and acknowledge the Biblical proof showing us satan's evil character with whom we really have to deal with every single day, so we're not caught off guard!

The **second source** showing us the character of satan is **The Societal Proof.**

Once again this is a common-sense question but let me pose it anyway. "If satan is real and really rotten to the core, as the Bible clearly shows all over the place, Old and New Testament, and satan hasn't been destroyed yet, then he's probably still spreading his evil across the planet today." How many of you can figure that out without any help? Well guess what folks? That's exactly what we find all throughout our society when you look around. Satan is not just real, but he really is permeating his evil character across our planet getting people to emulate him, look like him, and even act like him, as much as he can, with what time he has left. That's how evil he is.

And there's a multitude of ways he's doing that today, but I only have time to deal with one of them and that's the media. As we saw previously, in satan's fall in Isaiah 14, satan wanted to be God, he wanted to be worshipped like God. But he lost because the position isn't open. But that's when he went after us, mankind. He hates us! The reason he hates us is because we are created in the image of God and that's what satan lost out on. He wanted to be God. He wanted us to worship him as god. He wanted people to reflect his image, not God's. Believe it or not, he's still up to that same evil deed today and he's using modern technology to get the job done! He's using the power of the mass media to get us, even Christians, to reflect his evil image, his evil character, not the character of God.

The **first way** he's doing that with the media is by **bombarding us with devilish behavior.** Over and over and over again, in the media, until we crack, and start to look just like him. That's part of his deceitful character.

Revelation 12:9 "Who is called the devil and satan, who deceives the whole world."

How does he do this? With the media. The global mass media. He gets people to think that the media has no effect on them when it really does. He deceives them! This is why advertisers spend billions of dollars every year on the media. They know they're going to get their billions of dollars back and a whole bunch more because the media really has an effect on our beliefs, buying habits, even our behavior. Let's take a look at that power:

THE POWER OF THE MEDIA

Calvin Coolidge (The 30th President of the U.S. 1923-1929) stated about the power of media even in his day, "It is the most potent influence in adapting and *changing the habits and modes of life...affecting what we eat, what we wear, and the work and play of a whole nation."*

"TV is not an art form or a cultural channel; it is an advertising medium...it seems a bit churlish and un-American of people who watch television to complain that their shows are lousy. They are not supposed to be any good. They are supposed to make money."

"Every day, consumers are exposed to no less than 1000 commercial messages."

"The name 'Hollywood' was carefully chosen as the name for the newly established motion picture industry in the 1920's. In ancient witchcraft, the most powerful wood for a witch or wizard to make a magic wand, was from the Holly tree. Thus, the most powerful magicians always used a Hollywood magic wand. And one of the things they used the wand made of 'holly' wood for was to 'mesmerize' people."

"The average person spends 4½ hours a day watching TV which is enough time to read the Bible 22 times in just one year.³

Looks like we're "mesmerized" by the media and somebody's using it to lead us away from God! I wonder who that might be? And again, it's not just to get us "mesmerized" with it and lead us away from God, it's to get us to act like the devil himself. Here's what he's getting us to put in our brains:

SEX & VIOLENCE IN THE MEDIA

- The average American adolescent will view nearly 14,000 sexual references on TV per year.
- 75% of prime-time network shows included sexual content, up 67% in one year alone.
- Nearly one third of family hour shows contain sexual references.
- And it's about to get worse! They're now working on full-blown nudity shows! "Seven shows right now are being rolled out that feature complete nudity." Not just showing nudity here and there, that's bad enough, it's complete full-blown nudity all the time!
- MTV has a couple new shows out, one is called "Virgin Territory" where participants are trying to lose their virginity or what they call V-Card. Another show is called, "Happyland" where there is a teen story line that promotes

incest. And the lead person playing the girl in the show said, "Incest is hot and we're going to have fun!" on TV!
- And if you think that's bad now, it's getting so bad that their airing commercials on TV promoting adultery.

Prime News, CNN, Happening Now says, *"We certainly don't need commercials to get us to cheat on our spouse. Like this ad campaign by this Pro-adultery site, An Affair to Remember. But they are out there in your face ads and your kids can even see this*

Two couples are getting married, they look so happy. But the next screen shows she is with her husband's best friend and he is with some other woman. Or maybe it was her with her co-worker and him with her best friend. The ad says, 'Isn't it about time to have an affair, Life is short, have an affair, go to AshleyMadison.com'.

Look how happy he is looking up the website and wow she is even happier searching for someone to have an affair with. He can't wait to get into his car to go pick her up and off to the Hotel. The music is playing, there's nothing I haven't tried. 'Shhhhhh, Ashley Madison'. Life is short, have an affair.

That's the tag line for AshleyMadison.com. An online dating service for married people advocating adultery."

- The average American child or teenager views 10,000 murders, rapes, and aggravated assaults per year on television.
- 80.3 percent of all television programs contain acts of violence.
- A child born today will witness 200,000 acts of violence on television by the time they are eighteen.

- And the question more and more concerning parents and public officials is this: What is all this viewing doing to them?[4]

Gee, I wonder? But don't worry, we all know the deceitful lie that this has no effect on us whatsoever. It's just Entertainment, right? Yeah right! Again, advertisers spent 5-5 ½ million dollars last year alone on a 30 second Super Bowl Commercial…because we all know they have a lot of money to waste![5] No! It's because they know it's going to affect our behavior and it has! Here's how this devilish media has affected our behavior and got us to act like the Devil himself:

SEX & VIOLENCE IN OUR BEHAVIOR

- Approximately one-third of the entire population of the United States (110 million people) currently has a sexually transmitted disease according to the Centers for Disease Control and Prevention.
- Every single year, there are 20 million new cases of STD in America.
- America has the highest STD infection rate in the entire industrialized world.
- The United States has the highest teen pregnancy rate in the entire industrialized world.
- For women under the age of 30, more than half of all babies are being born out of wedlock.
- In the United States today, more than half of all couples "move in together" before they get married.
- The marriage rate in the United States has fallen to an all-time low. 6.8 marriages per 1,000 people.
- And because of that America has one of the highest divorce rate in the world.
- And we also have one of the highest percentage of one person households on the entire planet.
- One out of every three children in the United States lives in a home without a father.
- 69% of Americans believe there's nothing wrong with divorce.
- 67% of Americans believe sex outside of marriage is perfectly fine.
- 58% of American believe having a baby outside of marriage is fine.
- 72% of Americans believe gay and lesbians relations are fine.
- A high school kid took two kitchen knives went on a stabbing rampage through his school.
- A Florida teen was accused of poisoning the teacher's drink.
- A father put his 6-week-old daughter in a freezer to keep her from crying.

- Three children were left to starve to death while one was chained to the floor.
- A woman was arrested after police say she injected hand sanitizer into the feeding tube of her infant son.
- Florida parents were arrested after abandoning their three kids in the Woods
- A grandmother forced soiled underwear down her 11-year-old granddaughter's mouth.
- A caregiver used a stun gun to punish kids.
- A couple locked their 3-year-old child in the trunk to cure his fear of darkness.
- A mother stabbed her baby in an attempted murder-suicide.
- A woman strangled her newborn son and tossed him in trash.
- A dad killed his kids and wife 'because he didn't have car seats.'
- A Texas man was convicted of murdering his neighbors over dog feces.
- A pregnant woman attacked her roommate over butter.
- A North Miami Beach man was fatally shot after a fight over utensils breaks out at Baptism party.
- A Florida man bites his neighbor's ear off over a cigarette.
- A man stabbed a woman for bringing home pizza instead of a chicken sandwich.[6]

How many of you would say that's some serious, rotten, evil, devilish, behavior there! Yeah. And I wonder where it all came from? This is all part of satan's deceit. He's a deceiver. He gets us to think that the media exists to give us entertainment and fun, when in reality it's his high-tech tool in the last days to get us to emulate his character, not God's. He knows the rule, junk in equals junk out! Monkey see, Monkey do! Devil plays in the media, people will do, even Christians!

The **second way** satan gets us to emulate his character with the media is by bombarding us with **devilish practices**.

I'm talking about the occult. It's bad enough that he uses the media to get us to behave like him, but he uses the same media to get us to engage in his practices as well. That's all part of his lies. That's why he's called the father of them.

John 8:44 "You belong to your father, the devil…he is a liar and the father of lies."

And this is another one of his biggest lies. He gets us to think his dark occult practices are something harmless when in reality it's evil repackaged and he's using the media to promote it! Don't believe me? All he's done with just one of his evil practices called witchcraft, is to change the name to Wicca. That's all he's done. It's just old-fashioned witchcraft repackaged. Then he makes it appear as if it's something good for the environment and people are falling for it, right and left, especially teenagers. Witchcraft says that in order to contact the gods and goddesses, which are demons, for personal power, you need to practice astrology, divination, incantations, psychic power, and speaking with the dead. These are the same shows satan is promoting in the media right now. Shows like "Psychic Hotline" or "Crossing Over" with John Edwards, or the latest one with that lady in New Jersey called, "Long Island Medium," "Charmed" and "Twilight" and the "Harry Potter" series, which is making witchcraft look good to the kids. Don't believe me? Let's listen to their words. They're more honest than we are:

THE EFFECT OF HARRY POTTER ON KIDS

"J.K. Rowling, the author of the Harry Potter Series admitted she got many requests from children that wanted to attend Hogwarts school of witchcraft and wizardry. And we know, from books that are out there and with interviews of children, that they really wonder at night while they are lying awake if there is a Hogwarts that they can go to.

If you go to the Warner Brothers sight they ask you to enlist into Hogwarts while there are sights out there that are pulling in your children who are interested in learning more in various schools of witchcraft and wizardry.

The Association of Teachers and Lecturers tell us, 'This goes far beyond a case of reading a Harry Potter story. This represents an extremely worrying trend among young people.'

10-year-old Dylan: I want to go to wizard school and learn magic. I'd like to learn to use a wand to cast spells.

12-year-old, Mara: If I could go to wizard

school, I might be able to do spells and potions and fly a broomstick.

11-year-old Jeffrey: It would be great to be a wizard because you could control situations and things like teachers.

9-year-old Catherine: I'd like to go to wizard school, learn magic and put spells on people. I'd make up an ugly spell, and then it's payback time.

10-year-old Carolyn: I feel like I'm inside Harry's world. If I went to wizard school, I'd study everything: spell, counter spells, and defense against the Dark Arts.

13-year-old Julie: I liked it when the bad guys killed Unicorn and Voldemort drank its blood.

11-year-old Nurya: The books are very clever. I couldn't put them down. When I was scared I made myself believe it was supposed to be funny, so I wasn't too scared."[7]

Yeah, very clever, isn't it? Satan is indoctrinating kids into the dark arts of witchcraft through the media and people don't think it affects them when it does! No wonder he's called the deceiver! In fact, those kids who grew up watching Harry Potter, are now going into the military, and there's so many of them that are now full-blown witches, that the military is allowing them to have their own witchcraft services:

"Eyewitness News – Ken's 5 reports that Halloween may mean costumes and candy for you and for us but for those out there that are witches, it is their most sacred holiday.

In San Antonio, there is a Wiccan coven touting the largest weekly service for the study of witchcraft in the world. Where they meet and who is in the class may surprise you. Marvin Hurst has their story

'Mention the word witch and instantly most conjure a thought of black magic rituals and the belly of seclusion.'

'Just keep the line progressing,' says a soldier coming out of the Arnold Hall Community Center in San Antonio, Lackland.

'It's a different picture.' Says the reporter.

'My name is Archer, and I am a witch.' Says the man in black talking to a room full of soldiers.

'Archer, AKA Tony Gatland, is the high priest of this Coven, a packed house where the basic military trainees are studying witchcraft in his circle.' Says the reporter.

Archer explains, 'When we come over here on a Sunday, often there are 3 or 4 hundred.'

About 320 this day taking part in Samhain, the witches New Year celebration on Halloween, they honor the death and rebirth of their god. Trainees literally line up by choice to learn about Wicca. Fantasy reading of Harry Potter.

One soldier who joined in 5 years ago says, 'There is nothing wrong with Wicca and of course that is why we have this service here.'"[8]

Looks to me like all this Media Promotion of Witchcraft through Harry Potter really does have an effect on people…shocker! In fact, so does the Twilight series. That's another one! People not only want to become a Witch, but now a Vampire:

Watching her children in a playground in Guadalajara, Mexico, Maria Jose Cristerna is just an ordinary mom. But with her distinctive look she is likely to attract more attention than from her

peers. She's made several dramatic modifications to her body to transform herself into Vampire Woman.

Maria is 98% covered in tattoos, she's also had dental implants to give her fangs and titanium horns placed in her skull. Maria has given up her job as a lawyer to open a tattoo parlor and clothes shop. She insists her life is no different from any other wife and mothers.[9]

Yup, all this media and promotion of occult practices with witchcraft and vampirism has no effect whatsoever on people, it's just entertainment it's no big deal, and what's satan called? The Great Deceiver! But if you don't want to listen to me, then listen to the witches. Even they admit that because of this media promotion of their occult practices, "It's got people to no longer be afraid of it, even in the Church."

"Quotes from witches and warlocks are as follows:

'Fear has gone out of the general public; the craft is more and more acceptable.'

'Paganism has infiltrated the main stream thought pattern of most American's today.'

'There is a pagan revival. There are more people practicing true paganism than there are practicing true Christianity.'

'Many people are seeking something apart from Christianity. The thing that attracts young people is the power. And its immediate power.'

'As you see in the movie Twilight the vampire asks the girl he has met if she is afraid of him. Her reply is 'No.' We are conditioned to believe that vampires are more romantic than something to fear.'

'Whenever you drink blood you gain incredible power.'

'Magic is about getting what you want. Magicians are people that get what they want.'

'Slowly but surely the beauty of this is becoming wide spread.'

'Psychic vampirism and physical vampirism is a way of achieving power through black magic.'

'In the movie, the Crow, we see the vampire announcing to the public that he feels it is time to come forward and introduce himself. All the media is there to record the whole production to send to the world.'

A witch proclaims, 'I am very proud to be a witch.'

Another says, 'We live in a post Christian era and we are moving towards a neo paganism. The neo pagan revival has proceeded so rapidly and they have had the cooperation of the media in getting their message spread.'

'They claim that a lot of what they do has been taken over by the Church. The Church has married into occult practices. They no longer know the difference as they become desensitized to the things of evil.'[10]

People should be very concerned instead of allowing themselves to become desensitized because all this media promotion of Witchcraft, Vampirism, and the Occult is designed to destroy you and your family and because of this media promotion, many are now saying that Wicca is now the fastest growing religion in the U.S. and the second most popular among teens.[11]

Gee, I wonder why? What's satan called again? The Deceiver! He's got us thinking that the media exists to give us entertainment and fun, when in reality it's his high-tech tool in the last days to get us to emulate his evil character, not God's. He knows the rule. Junk in equals junk out! Promote the occult, people, even Christians, will do!

The third way satan gets us to emulate his character with the media is by bombarding us with **Devilish Acceptance**.

And what I mean by that is this. He not only wants us to behave like Him and engage in his evil practices, but he even wants us to look like him and even call him a good guy when he's not.

2 Corinthians 11:14 "And no wonder, for satan himself masquerades as an angel of light."

This is what he's doing with the media today! He's transforming his evil character into a so-called "angel of light" to get us to think he's a good guy who's just here to help us, instead of an evil satanic adversary with whom we have to deal! Don't believe me? Here's just one of the shows out there transforming the devil into a good guy. It's called "Lucifer."

In the trailer of the new Lucifer show we find Lucifer driving his hot car down the road, the clip says, "What would happen if Lucifer quit and moved to the city of angels?" He is no longer the bad guy. Now he brings out people's most forbidden desires.

Lucifer says, "People like to tell me things, their deep dark naughty desires that are on their minds." At a wedding he asks, "You're not marrying this human stain. You're not actually in love with him?" And she answers, "God no! I can't believe I just said that." He replies, "It must be something about his face."

Another clip: He asks a girl at a bar, "Can I have your autograph?" She asks, "Can I sell my soul to the devil?" Lucifer replies, "So the devil made you do it, did he, the alcohol, drugs, the topless selfies, the choices are on you my dear."

In another clip: "Someone out there should be punished," he says. Another girl replies, "Stop caring, you are the devil."

And another clip: A demon shows up to take him back to Hell. The waitress says, "I think you have a visitor." The demon says, "Your return to the underworld has been requested." Lucifer replies, "Let me check my calendar, it says the 7th through never to the 15th of ain't going to happen. How does that work for you guys?" The demon puts his claws to Lucifers' throat and Lucifer asks, "Do you think father is upset now?" The demon replies, "He's not going to be merciful for much longer."

But now he is a good guy, he thinks he should be out there punishing people that are responsible for their wrong doings. In another clip: At another time a girl asks him, "How can you possibly help me?" He answers, "I have the ability to draw out peoples forbidden desires."

And the final clip shows Lucifer talking to a little girl asking Lucifer, "What's your name?" He answers, "Lucifer." She asks, "The devil?" He answers, "Exactly."[12]

    Yeah, nice show for kids to watch. But don't you guys get it? Lucifer is just a good guy getting a bad rap from those nasty fundamentalist Christians when in reality he's just here to help us and solve crimes! Yeah right. It would be a crime to believe that lie! But he's not just going after the adults. He's also simultaneously going after the kids as well with the media trying to get them to think he's a good guy too. This is an excerpt from the show called "Childhood's End."

"As everyone is watching either by TV or congregated in a crowd in the auditorium the speaker comes on and says, 'Let the children come forth.'

Two small children proceed up the stairs to a bright light that engulfs them.

Everyone watches without making a move. They are mesmerized. The light gets brighter as they try to shade their eyes but out of the light comes a shadow. As they keep watching the shadow gets larger and then they see two large hoofed feet coming down the stairs with the two small children on each side.

As they get closer to the crowd they see that the hoofed creature has large wings, horns, and is about 8 feet tall. The children are looking up at this creature with smiles on their faces.

He lowers his wings and as the camera zeros in on his face the people watching by TV and in the auditorium, start gasping and covering their faces. It is the devil.

'Hello,' he says. 'There is no need to be afraid.' The crowd relaxes.

One couple, while watching in their living room, she says, 'He was right to hide himself from us. This world will be ok, won't it?' Her husband says, 'Yes I think so.'".[13]

See, that's just like those Baphomet Statues of Satan that Satanists are putting up in our Government buildings across America with kids looking up to him as a source of inspiration. He's a good guy, right? And what's the Bible say? He masquerades as an angel of light. He gets people to think he's good when he's not. But don't worry, we know all this media promotion of the Devil being a good guy has no effect on us, right? Well, you might want to tell that to this guy:

"Well, this guy wants to look like the devil. His name is Diablo Delenfer and to complete this dramatic look, he has had his teeth grinded to points, he's got his eyeballs tattooed so they are no longer white, they are red,

He's also had his tongue split in half. He has inserted metal balls into his forehead and he is also going through with an operation to place metallic balls to form a mohawk on the top of his head.

Tattoos cover him head to toe, I guess all he needs now is a pitchfork.

Another piece of interesting information about Diablo is when he goes under the knife under the needle to get this stuff done, none of its regulated, it's all classified as body modification, so he does it without the anesthetic. I can't imagine that eyeball procedure was fun.

Diablo Delenfer isn't his real name. He adopted that name while going through all this change. He was born Gavin Paslo. But he got me thinking there are so many other names he could have adopted, he could have gone all the way out and called himself St Lucifer, Beelzebub, if you open the Bible, that ones in there or the tempting serpent.

He continues to push forward, coming up with whatever he can to get that look fully completed and the final step for him is he says he wants a tail. And not just some prosthetic piece you get at the Halloween shop. He wants an organic one. Something that kind of waves behind him. What's he going to do after that? Is he going to get hooves?"[14]

    Nosiree, none of this media has any effect on us. It's all entertainment, it's harmless, when the deceitful lying masquerading one knows better. He's using the power of the mass media in these last days as his high-tech tool to get us, young and old alike, to now accept him as a good guy and even want to look like him. Can you believe this? Folks, it's high time we get our head out of the sand and deal with the war we are in! If you're reading this today and you're not saved, you better wake up and deal with reality. The devil is not only real, but he's really using the power of the mass media to get you to emulate his image and join him in the Lake of Fire.

    But Church, when are we going to stop being ignorant of the devil's schemes and stop being brainwashed by the media ourselves! We need to shut this stuff off and start emulating God's Character and lead the way back! Amen? This is not a game! There's a war going on and it's not just abroad but its right here in our own country. It's a cosmic battle for the souls of men and women all around us. The stakes are high, and millions of lives are at risk. If we're ever going to win this war, then the American Church needs to once again shine for Jesus Christ and take this seriously! This is no time to be ignoring the character of satan! We need to wake up Church! The alarm has sounded. We are under attack, it's *the Satanic War on the Christian.* Don't let the enemy get you! Amen?

Chapter Four

The Character of Demons

"It wasn't the first time the U.S. took on the greatest naval power in the world and here we were at it again only 36 years after declaring our Independence from these same people.

Great Britain, once again, not only attempted to restrict our country' trade, but they even 'impressed' or in other words forcibly place our American men into their service, essentially arresting them and placing them into their Navy.

Can you believe that? Well that was it! The Battle was on!

And even though the United States suffered many costly defeats at the hands of British, Canadian and Native American troops, including the capture and burning of our nation's capital, and the White House, in Washington, D.C., nonetheless, the American troops were able to repulse the British invasions in New York, Baltimore and even at the Battle of New Orleans.

And after three years of fighting, the war was finally ended with the signing of the Treaty of Ghent in Belgium, and it was not only being called the 'Second War of Independence' for America, but for some reason it's not really remembered in Great Britain today.

In fact, this same war actually inspired the song that would eventually become our National anthem, "The Star-Spangled Banner."

O say can you see, by the dawn's early light,
What so proudly we hailed at the twilight's last gleaming,
Whose broad stripes and bright stars through the perilous fight,
O'er the ramparts we watched, were so gallantly streaming?

And the rockets' red glare, the bombs bursting in air,
Gave proof through the night that our flag was still there;
O say does that star-spangled banner yet wave
O'er the land of the free and the home of the brave?[1]

The date was 1812-1815. The War was called The War of 1812."[1]

  Now folks, how many of you have heard of the Battle of 1812? I think most of us have. And how many of you would say that battle was a very important battle in the history of our country? But with all due respect to those who lost their lives in the Battle of 1812, what if I were to tell you that I know of a battle that makes The Battle of 1812 look like a backyard picnic? And what if I were to tell you that this battle didn't occur in just one place and one country at one time, but it's going on right now today all over the world and it's been leaving a trail of death and destruction for centuries. Folks, I'm talking once again about *the Satanic War on the Christian.*

  We Christians don't battle here and there once in a while. We go to war, every single day. Whether you see it, feel it, believe it or not, the moment you got saved you entered a spiritual war against a demonic host whose sole purpose is to destroy you and extinguish your testimony for Jesus Christ. And what's wild is that most wars go on for a few years or even longer. But *the Satanic War on the Christian* has been going on for the last 2,000 years non-stop and it's sending people straight into hell! And what's wild is most people will readily talk about all the other wars throughout history and all their atrocities, and rightly so, we have the History Channel, we need to talk about them! Yet how many people, even Christians, will openly discuss the longest war in mankind's history, *the Satanic War on the Christian* that has destroyed more lives than all the wars put together? Therefore, in order to stop getting duped and beat up all over the place, we're going to continue in our study, *the Satanic War on the Christian.*

Now so far, we've seen if you're ever going to win a war, then the **first thing** you must do is **Know Who Your Enemy Is.**

The **second thing** you need to know is **What Your Enemy is Like**, their character, amen?

It's common sense, right? And there we saw that the character of satan was evil, rotten, deceptive to the core! You don't want to mess with him! But that was the problem. We not only don't know who our enemy is because we refuse to believe in him, but we don't even know what we're up against because nobody wants to deal with his evil character. When the whole time, the Biblical proof & the Societal proof is screaming out to us, "Are you nuts! Look around! Why do you think the world is so messed up?" Proof of satan's evil character permeating our planet is everywhere, getting people to emulate him, look like him, act like him, and even change their appearance to resemble him, as much as they can, with what time they have left. That's how evil he is. And we saw he's doing that in the media. His high-tech tool in the last days to get us to emulate his character, not God's. But that's not all.

The **second character** we need to deal with, if we're going to stop getting beat up and duped all over the place as Christians, in this *Satanic War on the Christian* is **the Character of Demons.**

Satan is not the only one permeating his evil character across our planet today messing things up. So are his evil horde of demons that aid him in his evil attacks against us. They too are spreading their evil character!

Revelation 16:1-14 "Then I heard a loud voice from the temple saying to the seven angels, 'Go, pour out the seven bowls of God's wrath on the earth.' The first angel went and poured out his bowl on the land, and ugly and painful sores broke out on the people who had the mark of the beast and worshiped his image. The second angel poured out his bowl on the sea, and it turned into blood like that of a dead man, and every living thing in the sea died. The third angel poured out his bowl on the rivers and springs of water, and they became blood. Then I heard the angel in charge of the waters say: 'You are just in these judgments, You Who are and Who were, the Holy One, because You have so judged; for they have shed the blood of Your saints and prophets, and You have given them blood to drink as they deserve.' And I heard the altar respond: 'Yes, Lord God Almighty, true and just are Your judgments.' The fourth angel poured out his bowl on the sun, and the sun was given power to scorch people with fire. They were seared by the intense heat and they cursed the name of God, who had control over these plagues, but they refused to repent and glorify Him. The fifth angel poured out his bowl on the throne of the beast, and his kingdom was plunged into darkness. Men gnawed their tongues in agony and cursed the God of heaven because of their pains and their sores, but they refused to repent of what they had done. The sixth angel poured out his bowl on the great river Euphrates, and its water was dried up to prepare the way for the kings from the East. Then I saw three evil spirits that looked like frogs; they came out of the mouth of the dragon, out of the mouth of the beast and out of the mouth of the false prophet. They are spirits of demons performing miraculous signs, and they go out to the kings of the whole world, to gather them for the battle on the great day of God Almighty."

Now folks, maybe it's just me, but how many of you guys would say that the 7-year Tribulation is one place you don't want to be? Yeah, slightly! It's the worst time in the history of mankind, as Jesus said. What makes it so horrible, as we saw, not only is God's wrath being poured out upon this wicked and rebellious planet, because they refused to repent, it didn't have to be that way, but on top of that, satan, the antichrist, the false prophet, and demonic spirits were deceiving people into doing the dumbest thing ever, trying to take on God at the Battle of Armageddon and defeat Him. Like that would ever happen! How many guys would say that's pretty dumb? That's deceptive! But this is the point. This one passage alone gives us an insight into the evil rotten deceptive character that demons really have, just like satan, the antichrist, and the false prophet.

But this is the problem! People, even in the Church, are not only denying the existence of satan and demons, but because of that, they never get around to understanding their evil character either, so they don't know what they're up against! And again, if you're ever going to win a war you have to know what you're up against, right? What is the character of your enemy! What are they like? What are they up to? It's common sense, right? So that's what we're going to do now. We're going to take a look at the character of demons, so we don't get blindsided by their attacks either, amen?

The **first and primary source** showing us the character of demons is **The Biblical Proof.**

Believe it or not folks, Revelation 16 is just one of many passages in the Bible that reveals to us the character of demons, over and over again, in whom we really have to deal with. There really is a war going on! Old Testament, New Testament, their character is mentioned all over the place, so we don't get caught off guard. They are flat out evil! Let's take a look at some of that proof.

THE CHARACTER OF DEMONS

- Intelligent – Mark 1:24
- Know Their Doom – Matthew 8:29
- Know the Plan of Salvation – James 2:19
- Know the Deity of Jesus – Matthew 8:29/Mark 1:23
- Seek to Hinder the Plan of God – Daniel 10:10-14/Revelation 16:13-16
- Promote Satan's Program in Opposing God – Revelation 12:7
- Promote Rebellion – Genesis 3
- Promote Idolatry – Leviticus 17:7
- Promote False Religions – 1 John 4:1-4
- Torment & Oppress People – 1 Samuel 16
- Wage War on Believers – Ephesians 6:10-18
- Inflict Problems on Believers – Job ½ Corinthians 12:7
- Work in Numbers – Matthew 12:45
- Work as a Team – Ephesians 6:12
- Tempt to Sin – Ephesians 2:1-3
- Persecute – Revelation 12:13
- Prevent Service – 1 Thessalonians 2:18
- Disturb the Church – 2 Corinthians 2:10-11
- Cause Trouble – Judges 9:23
- Cause Selfishness & Divisions in the Church – James 3:13-16
- Cause Mental Disorders – Luke 8:27-29
- Cause Irrational Behavior – Luke 8:27-29

- Cause Suicidal Mania – Mark 9:22
- Inflict Illnesses – Matthew 9:33/Luke 13:11-16
- Inflict Physical Harm – Acts 19:13-16
- Possess Animals – Mark 5:13
- Promote False Doctrine – 1 Timothy 4:1
- Spirit Behind False Prophets – 1 Kings 22:21-23
- Influence Nations – Isaiah 14/Ezekiel 28/Daniel 10:13/Revelation 16:13-14
- Possess Unbelievers – Matthew 9:32/Mark 6:13[2]

Now folks, maybe it's just me, but I'm kind of thinking that the Bible emphatically declares that real live actual wicked entities called demons, evil spirits, unclean spirits, really do exist. Anybody? Their character is evil and rotten to the core, right? They are not a joke and you don't want to mess with them! And that was just 30 descriptions of their character, that's not all of them! Old Testament, New Testament from the beginning to the end, their character is revealed to us over and over again, so we don't get caught off guard! They are real and they're really evil and rotten to the core! God wants us to know their character, so we're not caught off guard, we know what we're up against, and so we don't get blindsided!

So, this is point. How in the world can you sit there and say as a supposed Christian that demons are not real, no big deal, nothing to worry about, it's just "a figment of your imagination," "a mere symbol of evil," when God tells us so much about them and how evil they really are for our own good! It's crazy! No wonder we're getting whooped on! We not only don't know who our 2nd Enemy is, because we refuse to believe in them, but we don't even know what we're up against, because nobody wants to deal with their evil character. We need to get our heads out of the sand and deal with reality!

The **second source** showing us the character of demons is **The Societal Proof.**

And once again this is a common-sense question but let me pose it anyway. If demons are real, and really rotten to the core, as the Bible clearly shows all over the place, Old and New Testament, and demons haven't been destroyed yet, then they're probably still spreading their evil character across the planet today. How many of you can figure that out without any help? Well guess what folks? That's exactly what we find all throughout our society when you look around. Demons are not just real, but they really are permeating their evil character across our planet getting people to emulate them, act like them, and even be possessed by them, non-Christians, as much as they can, with what time they have left. That's how evil they are.

And there's a multitude of ways they're doing that today, but I only have time to deal with one of them and that's the mind. Folks, the Bible is clear. The mind is one of the first places the enemy will always go to seek an entrance in our lives. There is a battle for our mind every single day when we get up. This is where the Spiritual War starts.

THE BATTLE OF THE MIND

The Enemy Blinds the Mind - 2 Corinthians 4:4 "The god of this age has blinded the minds of unbelievers, so that they cannot see the light of the gospel of the glory of Christ, who is the image of God."

We Seek to Recapture the Mind - 2 Corinthians 10:5 "We demolish arguments and every pretension that sets itself up against the knowledge of God, and we take captive every thought to make it obedient to Christ."

The Enemy Leads Astray/Destroys the Mind - 2 Corinthians 11:3 "But I am afraid that just as Eve was deceived by the serpent's cunning, your minds may somehow be led astray from your sincere and pure devotion to Christ."

We Seek to Re-Control the Mind – Philippians 4:7-8 "And the peace of God, which transcends all understanding, will guard your hearts and your minds in Christ Jesus. Finally, brothers, whatever is true, whatever is noble, whatever is right, whatever is pure, whatever is lovely, whatever is admirable – if anything is excellent or praiseworthy – think about such things."

Believe it or not, this is the same battle of the mind going on every single day spiritually, whether we realize it or not. Every day when you get out of bed, the enemy is seeking to control you, blind you, and even destroy you, if they can, all through the mind. And they attack us in the mind, even Christians, to reflect their evil image, their evil character, not the character of God, and even possess people if they can, that is the non-Christian, as we'll see in a moment.

The first way they're doing that with the mind is by **Seducing Us with Demonic Drugs**.

Folks, believe it or not, drugs are going to be one of the biggest ways the enemy gets people to be possessed by them in the last days!

Revelation 9:20,21 "The rest of mankind that were not killed by these plagues still did not repent of the work of their hands; they did not stop worshiping demons...nor did they repent of their murders, their magic arts, their sexual immorality or their thefts."

Notice the word there in the text, "magic arts." It said they did not repent of their "magic arts." It's actually the Greek word "pharmakeia" where we get the English word pharmacy from which literally means "drugs or drugging's" And so, this one-word, clues us in on the first reason why people in the last days are so stinking evil and refuse to repent and get right with God even though they're being judged by God. The Demons are going to be inspiring a massive amount of drug usage across the planet apparently clouding their minds in the last days.

But hey, good thing we don't see any signs of that happening anytime soon, yeah right! Turn on your TV man! What do we hear every single night? Drug this, drug that, drug problem here, drug raid there, drugs in schools, drugs in homes, drugs in streets, drugs in the government, drugs around the world, right? Drug usage has gone ballistic around the world and it's spawning all kinds of wicked behavior.

In fact, they're even creating new ones! They're called, "designer drugs." One of the latest ones is called, "Krokodil." And it's called "krokodil" because of what it does to people. It turns their skin greenish and scaly in appearance and eventually causes their blood vessels to rupture and kills the surrounding skin tissue. And this creates huge chunks of dead flesh to appear on their bodies, you know, kind of like a zombie creature, and I quote, "Once you're an addict at this level, (using this stuff), any rational thinking doesn't apply." Which, I would say,

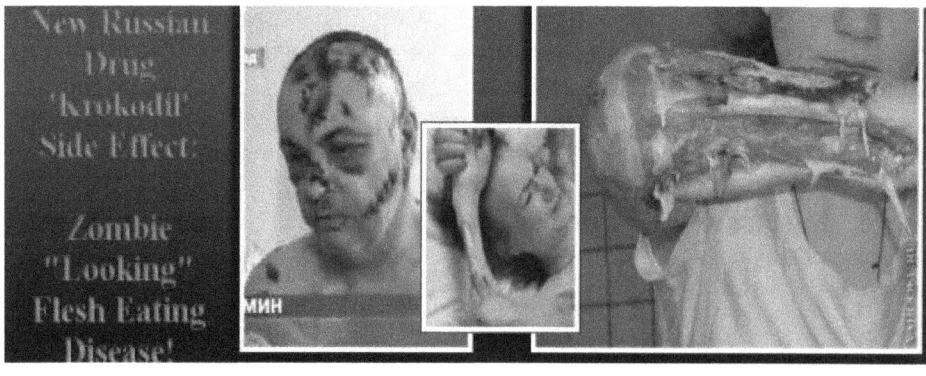

would include getting right with God in the midst of being judged by God, right? And speaking of zombies, there's the other new drug outbreak we keep hearing about? Bath salts, right? Of all things, bath salts, and what is it causing people to do? As we've seen on the news, it causes other people to eat people's faces off! Can you believe that? You talk about wicked behavior!

And folks, the experts are saying it going to get even worse. Why? Because there's another drug out there that is being legalized right now that the drug experts are saying is a gateway drug to using all different kinds of drugs, and that drug is Marijuana. And experts are saying, man, if that thing gets legalized, and it is, we ain't seen nothing yet! Drug usage is going to go nuts! It's a gateway drug. It's going to spawn all kinds of wicked behavior, even worse than what we see today!

In fact, it's already started. Studies have shown that since Marijuana has been legalized in certain areas that "crime rates have gone up" as well as "homelessness," AND it's causing more deaths, it's killing more people! "Pot Fuels Surge in Drugged Driving Deaths." It doesn't make them safer drivers! Are you kidding me! It makes them more dangerous drivers! We know it's going to increase even more, because now it's not only being legalized all over the place, but now they're making it so easy for you to get, that you can even get it in a Vending Machine.

And now this surge of drug usage has gone ballistic! "22 million people in the United States are already using illegal drugs," and it's only going to increase as you continue to "legalize" it. And according to the Federal Government, "The number of Heroin addicts in the United States has more than doubled since 2002." And "The number of Heroin-related deaths has risen 84% since 2010." And a recent report shared how junior high girls are now doing

Crystal Meth, in school![3] Well gee, I wonder why? You keep legalizing this stuff and you put it in vending machines and you reap what you sow! It all spills downhill! That's what the experts are saying!

But hey, good thing we don't see any signs of the Church having a part of this. Yeah, right! Here's how demonically deceived we are:

"Legalization of Marijuana has been sung about by Peter Tash but who would have thought that television evangelist Pat Robertson would now support the idea. Pat Robertson says, 'I became sort of a hero of the hippy culture, I guess, when I said I thought we should decriminalize the possession of marijuana.' But another group is using the law to start a brand-new church. In fact, church members say they love Cannabis. One member says, 'Not everyone is happy to have them in their southeast side of their neighborhood.'

'Others have a place but where is ours. The International Church of Cannabis is a 13,000-square foot space located in Denver Colorado that is the first large venue in the world where adults can legally consume cannabis in a social environment.

Our church is the spiritual home for adults everywhere who ritually take the sacred flower to find inspiration and meaning. We are Elevationists. An open-minded congregation that welcomes people of all faiths and cultures to join us as we partake of the sacred flower with you our brothers and sisters.'

They flock from as far away as Montana. One says, 'I've never seen a church like this and I used to smoke pot.'

'Welcome to the First Church of Cannabis,' says the leader.

'I hitchhiked 978 miles to get here and I'd do it all over again,' another member said.

The leader, Bill Levin, greeted one visitor who told him that he had traveled 1,000 miles to share love with you, WOW!"[4]

Wow is right! Who would've thought that a so-called Christian evangelist would be promoting the legalization of marijuana and now Churches are popping up all over the place using it in their so-called Worship services! And I get it, attendance is down, and people will drive hundreds of miles to join you but come on! This is demonic and deceptive! Why? Because what most people don't realize is that once you start using drugs, you don't just open physical doors, you open spiritual doors. You're not just taking a physical trip. You're taking a "spiritual" trip. Been there done that, wish I wouldn't have bought the T-shirt! You see, once you start using drugs it puts you into an "altered state of consciousness" and drugs by the way are just one of the ways you can do that.

Other ways include hypnotism by psychotherapist, repetitive movement, like what the Hindu Yogis encourage, repetitive speech like the Hare Krishnas do with repeating their mantras over and over again. Certain body postures and stretches like with Yoga, which mean to "Yoke," it's a movement to "yoke" yourself with the Hindu gods, i.e. demons, and various forms of breathing exercises and meditation. They all, including drugs, get you into an altered state of consciousness, and once you do that, you're not just doing something physically, you're doing something spiritually. You're opening yourself to demonic forces to come in and take control of you, like this man shares:

"No one knows what hypnosis is, no one knows what goes on in the mind, to alter the state of consciousness like Yogi's, witch doctors, have been practicing. It loosens the normal connection between your spirit and your brain.

Hypnotists can't control you, they can make all kinds of suggestions, make you think things are happening, that are not happening, make you think you have powers that you don't, experiences that you haven't had, even implant memories.

Other beings, that there are other minds out there, they could also do the same thing. Sir John Eckles, Nobel Prize winner for his research on the brain, describes the brain as 'a machine that a ghost can operate.'

What he means by that is your spirit operates your brain in a normal state of consciousness, in an altered state reached under Yoga, TM, or hypnosis, you have loosened your normal connection between your spirit and your brain and that allows other entities or other minds to interpose themselves and begin to tick off your neurons in your brain a universal illusion.

I believe is demonic. I think all the evidence indicates that."[5]

And I would agree. Let me get this straight. Drug usage as we've seen is on the rise all over the world, and it can cause people to do some pretty horrific things, like eating other people's faces off and now they're being legalized and used in so-called Church services and they can also open you up to be controlled by a demon? Gee, I wonder what kind of a society that's going to create? Welcome to the 7-year Tribulation! But is that really possible? Can drugs really open up the doors for people to get possessed? Well, you tell me if these people on this new drug called Flakka aren't demon possessed:

STFN News: *"A new synthetic killer drug is Flakka and it's is spreading rapidly across the United States and already causing an epidemic of overdose, fatalities and acts of violence.*

Flakka, some have called the insanity drug and its everywhere. It is the scariest drug in the world. More powerful than Heroin or Cocaine. It is a synthetic drug that can alter your state of mind, causing excited delirium, raising body temperature, and literally losing their mind.

They are exhibiting super human strength, that would take 6 policemen to hold them down. They have psychotic breakdowns, hallucinations, cannibalism, and self-mutilation, indiscriminate violence when Flakka takes over.

'We are living in the context of the End of the Age, we are a nation under judgement.' Welcome to state one of the Zombie apocalypses.

It's been long theorized that controlled substances could bring people closer to the spirit world. Sometimes what comes out of that experience isn't what you would expect.

Right now, our society is being plagued, dominated by an epidemic of controlled substances. In the 1970's people were talking about peace and love, but now people are coming back from bad trips and total psychosis. The number of over doses are up as are the cases of total zombification, i.e., demonic possession."[6]

      Hmmm. Maybe they really are preparing us for a dark horrible future with these Zombie movies. But nope! Demons aren't real! Drugs are no big deal, I'm just taking a physical trip, just having some fun. It's entertainment. I'll be fine! I can't get hurt. When the whole time it's the last days, demonic deception. They get us to think that drugs exist to give us entertainment and fun, when in reality it's their old-fashioned technique in the last days to get us to be possessed by them, the non-Christian, and emulate their evil character, not God's. They know the rule…blind the mind with drugs…cannot see the truth! Destroy the mind with drugs….and people…even Christians…will have no pure devotion to Christ…. they will only be devoted to them! They would not stop worshipping demons!
      The second way demons are getting us to emulate their evil character with the mind is by Seducing Us with Demonic Teaching that also happens to be pushing demonic drugs! That's another trick they pull off in the Last Days!

1 Timothy 4:1 "The Spirit clearly says that in later times some will abandon the faith and follow deceiving spirits and things taught by demons."

      But hey, that'll never happen, will it? Unfortunately, it already has, with the false demonic teaching of Secular Psychology! These guys, the Founders of

Secular Psychology, as we we'll see in a second, were not only involved in demonic practices and got their teachings straight from demons themselves, but they too push demonic drugs to get people in an altered state of consciousness to connect with demons. They along with the Big Pharma are the ones pushing this craze for "prescription drugs" that will mess people up!

And I say that because you hear people say, "Well, I don't use illegal drugs! I only use prescription drugs! I'm fine!" Well, just because it's legal, doesn't mean it's good for you! In fact, let's take a look at how many people are being drugged right now in the U.S:

STATISTICS ON DRUG USAGE

- According to a study conducted by the Mayo Clinic, nearly 70% of all Americans are on at least one prescription drug.
- An astounding 20% of all Americans are on at least five prescription drugs.
- Americans spend over 300 billion dollars on prescription drugs each year.
- Right now, there are 70 million Americans that are on mind-altering drugs of one form or another.
- In the United States today, prescription painkillers kill more Americans than heroin and cocaine combined.
- America has the highest rate of illegal drug use on the entire planet.[7]

Well, no wonder! You're pushing it all over the place! But folks, before I continue, I need to say I'm not against all forms of medication. Me personally, I'm glad they put a drug in me right before they cut me open and do surgery! Otherwise, I'd be lying there doing, "AAAHHH!!!" And I don't want to do that! But seriously, that's not what's going on here! Just because a drug is considered "legal" doesn't mean it's good for you OR that it won't open you up to demonic possession. In fact, secular experts are now admitting that some of these "mind-altering" drugs are altering people's behavior alright, it's turning them into the violent mindless criminals who are responsible for these latest demonic school shootings and massacres we've been seeing all over the place. I didn't say that they did:

CBN News Reports: *"The most violent outbreaks in the recent years have involved guns and new information indicates that there is often another common thread, antidepressants. From Columbine to Aurora, the Naval Yard to Ft. Hood, antidepressants have been linked to violence.*

Peter Breggin, Author of 'Medication Madness' has studied this. These drugs are causing agitation, anxiety, insomnia, hostility, aggression, mania.

'Antidepressants work on the brain thereby altering the way people think, in addition to driving the person with a nifedipine, the antidepressants do a bit of lobotomy, and you lose your empathy, you lose your caring.'

In his book Dr. Breggin sites real life examples of violence that could be blamed on antidepressants. 'An engineer who was given Paxil probably to help stop smoking or maybe for some tension, certainly not for any mental disorder. Within a couple of doses, he drowned his two children and himself in a tub.'"[8]

Well that sounds demonically inspired. Wonder why that happened? Because he was given a "legal" drug. But that doesn't mean it was good for you. And folks, is this really a surprise? Have you paid attention to these prescription drug commercials? I don't care if they are "legal" listen to the side-effects! It's supposed to cure your depression, but the side-effects are liver disease, heart disease, lung disease, typhoid, foot fungus, even more depression, thoughts of suicide, anger and rage, and it's spawning these killings! Excuse me? So, let's take a look at where these false demonic teaching came from, that we need drugs to cure everything, called Secular Psychology:

THE FOUNDERS OF SECULAR PSYCHOLOGY

- SIGMUND FREUD was an evolutionist who believed that man had evolved from lower animals and that the idea of an Almighty God was just a myth made up by our forefathers to cope with life and that "religion must be destroyed." Yet at the same time Freud was deeply involved in the occult and periodically consulted soothsayers, who were alleged to have telepathic powers. Not only was he an Honorary Fellow in the American Society  for Psychical Research but he even remarked that if he could live his life over, he would devote it to psychical research rather than psychoanalysis. Not only was he deep into the occult but he was extremely enthusiastic about the so-called positive health benefits of cocaine and was a user himself for many years to aid in his work. And that's not the only drug. Freud also had a severe addiction to nicotine to the tune of smoking an average 20 cigars a day, which eventually led to his death. But stir all this together and if one of main primary founders of Modern Secular Psychology had a severe drug problem and even thought dangerous drugs would somehow benefit others, then is it any wonder that Modern Psychology today is following in his footsteps by also pushing dangerous drugs as a so-called miracle?

- ABRAHAM MASLOW said that the motivation for his life's work was his absolute hatred of his mother. He also believed in order for people to be  fulfilled, "Self comes first (which is what Satan and Satanism teaches) and one needs to esteem themselves above all and meet all self needs first before they can love other people and have a fulfilling life."

  Yet the Bible says said the "greatest fulfilled life" is one who loves God first, then your neighbor second by esteeming them above yourself, and then denying yourself being willing to suffer if need be for God."

- KAREN HORNEY She suffered severe bouts of depression throughout her life and even attempted suicide. Later she got into Lesbianism and became interested in Zen, trying to see connection between psychological analysis and meditation.

- CARL JUNG made a wooden man out of a ruler that he called Manikin and kept it in a wooden case and frequently talked to it in times of trouble and even had a mystical experience while sitting on a rock where he couldn't tell if he was the rock or the rock was him. Then he later had what he considered a major breakthrough in life when he had a vision of God  supposedly going to the bathroom on a Church sanctuary from the sky.

However, what most people don't realize is that Carl Jung was also completely absorbed in the occult and studied their teachings, attending séances, listened to mediums, practiced necromancy, and had daily contact with disembodied spirits, which he called archetypes.

In fact, much of what he wrote was inspired by such entities, one of which he called Philemon. Listen to his own words: *"Philemon and other figures of my fantasies brought home to me the crucial insight that there are things in the psyche which I do not produce, but which produce themselves and have their own life. Philemon represented a force, which was not myself. In my fantasies, I held conversations with him, and he said things, which I had not consciously thought. For I observed clearly that it was he who spoke, not I. Philemon was a mysterious figure to me. I went walking up and down the garden with him, and to me he was what the Indians call a guru."*

Later he was contacted by another "spirit guide" called Basilides who "inspired" Jung to write his famous work, "The Seven Sermons to the Dead." Jung stated that the start of the work was very identical to a possession. *"Then it was as if my house began to be haunted. My eldest daughter saw a white figure passing through the room. My second daughter, independently of her elder sister, related that twice in the night her blanket had been snatched away; and that same night my nine-year-old son had an anxiety dream. Around five o'clock in the afternoon on Sunday the front doorbell began ringing frantically. It was a bright summer day; the two maids were in the kitchen, from which the open square outside the front door could be seen. Everyone immediately looked to see who was there, but there was no one in sight. I was sitting near the doorbell, and not only heard it but saw it moving. We all simply stared at one another."*

Over the next three evenings, the book was written, and as soon as he had begun to write, *"The whole ghostly assemblage evaporated. The room quieted, and the atmosphere cleared. The haunting was over."* Philemon and Basilides are just two of the 'spirit guides' that were in contact with Jung. The list of other guides also included one 'Salome.' In fact, Jung himself admitted: *"These conversations with the dead formed a kind of prelude to what I had to communicate to the world about the unconscious. All my works, all my creative activity, has come from those initial fantasies."* And that's why experts are now saying that it is clear that Jung's psychology makes him, in essence, the father of the New Age, giving a theoretical framework for channeling and other "New Age practices" and they are still pushing demonic, dangerous, murderous, drugs today.

STATISTICS ON PSYCHIATRY ABUSE

110 million people take Psychiatric drugs, 57 million in the U.S. alone, 4.4 billion dollars are spent on pharma advertising, marketing, manipulating, misleading. Here's what you won't see in the drug ads.

Psychiatric drugs cause: psychosis, mania, suicide, violence, homicide, death, stroke, rage, depression, diabetes, coma, aggression, impotence, amnesia, addiction, birth defects, weight gain, blackouts, 61,000 deaths, 19,000 birth defects, 25,000 suicides, 550 homicides, are attributed to psychiatric drugs each year while psycho pharma rakes in $88 billion every year, rakes in $7 billion every month, rakes in $1.7 billion every week, rakes in $246 million every day, $171 thousand every minute, on psychiatric drugs alone.

Question: Who commits more healthcare fraud? A) Hospital administrators, B) Medical doctors C) Psychiatrists? Answer: Psychiatrists, psychiatrists commit 40% of all healthcare fraud.

Question: Who involuntarily incarcerates the most citizens? A) Syria B) North Korea C) Psychiatrists? Answer: Psychiatric Institutions incarcerate 700,000 every year against their will.

Question: Who is the most Likely to die from electric shock? A) Electricians B) Victims of interrogation C) Psychiatric patients? Answer: Psychiatric patients receive 1 million shock treatments every year killing two per day.

Question: Where is a woman most likely to become a victim of rape? Answer: A) Public park B) College Campus C) Psychiatric ward? Answer: Psychiatric wards where 4 out of 10 women are raped

Question: What causes the most deaths in the Military? Answer: A) Enemy fire B) Accidents C) Suicide? Answer: Suicide, every day 23 soldiers & veterans take psychiatric drugs and kill themselves.

Question: Who is more likely to hook a minor on harmful drugs? A) Drug dealer B) Gang member C) Psychiatrist? Answer: Psychiatrist give 20 million children addictive drugs.

Question: Which of the following have the highest rate of arrest? A) Organized crime B) human trafficking C) Psychiatry? Answer: Psychiatrists: 1 in 5 are arrested on criminal charges.

Question: Who is most likely to molest your child? A) A stranger B) A registered sex offender C) A psychiatrist? Answer: A psychiatrist is 3 times more likely to sexually molest your child.

THE ANSWER IS CLEAR, HELP US ERADICATE PHYCHIATRIC ABUSE."[9]

Wow! Have we been duped by a demonic teaching in these last days or what? Looks to me like the Founders of Secular Psychology not only had some "psychological problems" themselves but they're teachings also came from demons and their demonic drugs invite more harm than good! Anybody else coming to that conclusion? In fact, what did the Paul say?

1 Timothy 4:1 "The Spirit clearly says that in later times some will abandon the faith and follow deceiving spirits and things taught by demons."

People today, even in the Church, will listen to a Psychologist over the Word not realizing that their teachings came from demons and their pushing of demonic drugs might actually be inviting even more demons! And who's the same entity that gets us to mock the existence of demons? Secular Psychology! "It's just a mental aberration." "It's a form of Psychosis." "Demons aren't real. We're much too sophisticated for that." And it's all part of the Last Days demonic deception. They get us to think that Drugs exist to give us better mental health and more joy, when in reality it's their old-fashioned technique in the last days to get us to be possessed by them, that is, the non-Christian and even emulate their dangerous, murderous, evil, psychotic character, not God's. They know the rule, blind the mind with drugs, even prescription ones, cannot see the truth! Destroy the mind with drugs, and people, even Christians, will have no pure devotion to Christ. They will only be devoted to them and their demonic false teachings!

Folks, it's is high time we get our head out of the sand and deal with the war we are in! If you're reading this today and you're not saved, you better wake up and deal with reality. Demons are not only real, but they're really using the seduction of the mind to get you to emulate their image and join them in the 'Lake of Fire.'

But Church, when in the world are we going to stop being ignorant of the devil's schemes and stop being seduced in our minds as well! We need to bring every thought captive and obedient to Christ and start emulating God's character and lead the way back! Amen? This is not a game! There's a war going on and it's not just abroad but its right here in our own country. It's a cosmic battle for the souls of men and women all around us. The stakes are high, and millions of lives are at risk. If we're ever going to win this war, then the American Church needs to once again shine for Jesus Christ and take this seriously! This is no time to be ignoring the character of demons! We need to wake up Church! The alarm has sounded. We are under attack, it's *the Satanic War on the Christian*. Don't let the enemy get you! Amen?

Chapter Five

The Tactic of Satan

"It was a typical Sunday morning with people eating breakfast and getting ready for Church services. And it appeared that the inhabitants of this island were going to be blessed with yet another beautiful sunny day.

But all that was to change in a matter of seconds. At 7:55 AM, Logan Ramsey looked out his window and spied not a palm tree in this tropical paradise, but a plane. And normally this wouldn't have been an unusual sight except that this plane dropped a bomb.

For the next one and a half hours over 350 enemy planes bombarded this American base. The surprise was complete. The destruction made easy. Why?

Because not only was every single warning sign completely ignored, but the American planes were parked in neat rows creating a dive bombers dream come true.

In fact, ten minutes into the attack, a bomb crashed through the deck of one of the battleships and ripped the sides open like a tin can and within minutes the massive ship sunk to the bottom taking 1,300 men with it.

And when the smoke cleared, and the final explosion was silenced the damaged was assessed. More than 180 planes were obliterated, several ships were sunk and incinerated, and 2,343 people were annihilated.

It was a day that will live in infamy. The year was 1941. The attack of course, was on Pearl Harbor."[1]

Now folks, how many of you have heard of the Attack on Pearl Harbor? Hello, I think most of us have. And how many of you would say that it was one of the worst U.S. disasters of all time. But with all due respect to those who lost their lives in the Attack on Pearl Harbor, what if I were to tell you that I know of an attack that makes Pearl Harbor look like child's play. What if I were to tell you that this attack didn't occur in just one place and one country at one time, but it's going on right now today all over the world and it's been leaving a trail of death and destruction for centuries. I'm talking once again about *the Satanic War on the Christian.* The facts are these. We Christians don't battle here and there once in a while. We go to war, every single day. Whether you see it, feel it, believe it or not, the moment you got saved you entered a spiritual war against a demonic host whose sole purpose is to destroy you and extinguish your testimony for Jesus Christ. What's wild, is that most wars go on for a few years or even longer. But *the Satanic War on the Christian* has been going on for the last 2,000 years non-stop and it's sending people straight to hell! Most people will readily talk about all the other wars throughout history and all their atrocities, and rightly so, we have the History Channel, we need to talk about them! Yet how many people, even Christians, will openly discuss the longest war in mankind's history, *the Satanic War on the Christian* that has destroyed more lives than all the wars put together? Therefore, in order to stop getting duped and beat up all over the place, we're going to continue in our study, *the Satanic War on the Christian.*

Now so far, we've seen if you're ever going to win a war, **the first thing** you must do is **Know Who Your Enemy Is.**

The **second thing** you need to know is **What Your Enemy is Like,** their character, amen? It's common sense, right?

We saw that not only the character of satan, but the character of demons is also evil, rotten, deceptive to the core! You don't want to mess with them either! But that was the problem. We not only don't Know Who Our Enemy is Satan or demons, because we refuse to believe in them, but we don't even know what we're up against because nobody wants to deal with their evil character either. When the whole time, the Biblical proof and the Societal proof is screaming out to us, "Are you nuts! Look around! Why do you think the world is so messed up?" Proof of demon's evil character is permeating our planet is everywhere. Getting people to emulate them, act like them, and even be possessed by them, non-Christians, as much as they can, with what time they have left. That's how evil they are. We saw how they're doing that with the mind. They get us to think that drugs entering the mind exist to give us more joy or better mental health. When in reality, it's their old-fashioned technique, in the last days, to get us to be possessed by them, that is the non-Christian, and even emulate their dangerous, murderous, evil, psychotic character, not God's. But that's not all.

The third thing we need to deal with if we're going to stop getting beat up and duped all over the place, as Christians in This *satanic War on the Christian* is **The Tactic of Our Enemy**.

That's right folks, you not only need to know who your enemy is and what they're like, but you also need to know what they're up to, what's their goal, why are they here, why are they doing what they're doing? Why in the world are we in a war in the first place? And folks, the tactics of satan are not good. In fact, he's very methodical about them!

Ephesians 6:10-13 "Finally, be strong in the Lord and in His mighty power. Put on the full armor of God so that you can take your stand against the devil's schemes. For our struggle is not against flesh and blood, but against the rulers, against the authorities, against the powers of this dark world and against the spiritual forces of evil in the heavenly realms. Therefore, put on the full armor of God, so that when the day of evil comes, you may be able to stand your ground, and after you have done everything, to stand."

Now folks, the Bible not only assumes that we as Christians are well aware of the struggle, the battle, the war, whatever you want to call it, we are in every single day, as Christians, but it also tells us that we need to put on the full Armor of God and be prepared for it, right? In fact, it even says we are to be prepared to take our stand against whose schemes? The devil's schemes! He really exists and he's really out to get us! In fact, the word scheming to get us, is the Greek word "methodeia" as in "methodology" or "methodical" and it speaks of his "well organized, ordered, planned, methodical, approach to get us, and to take us out, with his deceitful, cunning, evil trickery." In fact, the Bible says he's doing this in a multitude of ways:

THE TACTICS OF SATAN

- Provokes – 1 Chronicles 21:1
- Promotes Murder – John 8:44
- Promotes Lying – John 8:44
- Fills the Heart to Lie (Ananias) – Acts 5:3
- Causes Physical Illness – Job 2:7
- Causes Blindness – Luke 13:16
- Spiritually Blinds Unbelievers – 2 Corinthians 4:4
- Performs Powerful Signs, & Lying Wonders – 2 Thessalonians 2:9
- Shoots Flaming Arrows – Ephesians 6:6
- Hinders – 1 Thessalonians 2:18
- Condemns – 1 Timothy 3:6
- Snares – 1 Timothy 3:6
- Devours – 1 Peter 5:8
- Takes Away the Sown Word of God – Matthew 13:19
- Takes Advantage – 2 Corinthians 2:11
- Transforms – 2 Corinthians 11:14
- Tempts – Matthew 4:1
- Sifts People (Peter) – Luke 22:31
- Possess People (Judas) – John 13:2,27
- Casts into Prison – Revelation 2:10[2]

Maybe it's just me, but I'm kind of thinking that the Bible emphatically declares that real live, actual, wicked, devil is out to get us in a multitude of different ways every single day? His character is evil, his tactics are evil. Anybody? Yeah! He's scheming all over the place to get us. In fact, Paul also says we're not only to acknowledge this in Ephesians 6 and put on the full 'Armor of God', and be prepared, but the last thing you want to do is be unaware of this spiritual issue!

2 Corinthians 2:10-11 "If you forgive anyone, I also forgive him. And what I have forgiven – if there was anything to forgive – I have forgiven in the sight of Christ for your sake, in order that satan might not outwit us. For we are not unaware of his schemes."

That's the problem, isn't it? The Church today is unaware of the devil's schemes because they don't believe in him, and they don't even understand his character, let alone these actual real live evil tactics that he's using to get them. So now, because of that, he's right there in their midst, in the Church, trying to destroy them and they have no clue! Now tell me that's not a tactic of the devil! And that's the irony! To make sure we're not ignorant or unaware of the devil's schemes that are out to get us and destroy us, we're going to take a look at some of his evil tactics to come in and take us out.

The **first way** the devil seeks to destroy the Church is **by the followers of satan**. In other words, he seeks to infiltrate us, the Church, with Satanists. And you might think that's a pretty wild statement but folks we've already seen how they're increasing all over the country and now they're coming into the Church. Why? Because we don't believe in them anymore. Haven't you heard? It's just a figment of our imagination! It's just a scare tactic from Preachers. Therefore, they sneak right in under the radar without notice in the Church and they're here tearing things apart, destroying things, dividing us up into little pieces, as these former Satanists admit. It really goes on.

TESTIMONIES OF FORMER SATANISTS INVADING CHURCHES

Doreen, former Satanist/Black witch: *"Christians are Satanists worse enemies. They are out to torment you, they are out to blackmail you, they will even kill you. They tried to kill me, when I came out of black witchcraft."*

Bill Former Satanist: *"If you are in a church where the spirit of God is really moving and where the word is really being preached, and where prayer is really being brought up to Heaven, for the salvation of souls, then they are going to regard you as their mortal enemy and they are going to be out there trying everything they can destroy, to kill and to maim, because that is the nature of satan and that is also the nature of his followers. They will try and infiltrate your church, they will try and set up whispering campaigns against the pastor and the elders, they may even try to seduce the pastor."*

Glen former Satanist: *"For two years I was involved in the Baptist Church. I was constantly complaining about the Pastors sermons being too long, being too dry, sowing discord between the people, gossiping about others."*

Lady: *"As each member is initiated into the coven they are commissioned to do a job. One individual's job may be to desecrate a church."*

Jack Roper, Occult Researcher: *"They will destroy or desecrate churches, where they will spray paint the altar just to put fear into that Christian Church."*

Doreen says, *"Some Satanists are handpicked, the most powerful ones, and sent into churches to disrupt the meeting. We stopped people from going forward when they ask people to go forward to accept Christ as their Savior."*

Bill: *"I personally was trained to learn all the Christian jargon, Hallelujah, Praise the Lord, do all the right things and yet I had no more idea of Jesus being my savior as the man in the moon."*

Glen: *"If you can tear down the foundation of a church then you have destroyed that church and that's what every witch or Satanists want to do. Go into that church and tear down that prayer foundation and the rest of the church goes quickly after that."*

Bill: *"The real Satanist, the hard-core Satanists, are involved in criminal activity and for that reason they are going to try to look as normal as possible, so it will be easy to deceive you. They are doctors, lawyers, they're teachers, often times people in positions of great influence over small children."*

Policeman #1: *"Priest, ministers, police officers, judges, business men, gentlemen, teenagers, they are all linked together, to sacrifice whatever they want to Satan."*

Policeman #2: *"It would be a whole lot easier if these people wore horns, with a pitch fork and a red suit but they just don't, they could be your next-door neighbor."*[3]

Or the guy sitting right next to you in the pew. In fact, did you catch that part where he said it could even be a so-called Minister. Just because you went to Seminary doesn't mean you're saved. We'll deal with phony preachers and false brothers in just a little bit. But this is not the only thing going on, Satanists invading Churches to destroy them because that's the nature of satan and that's what his followers do, but the reports are coming out now to the Church to warn us of this "epidemic."

SATANISTS INVADING CHURCHES

"Presently, there are numerous reports that the entire structure of Christianity has been infiltrated by satanic people. This includes Pastorates, local Church leaders all the way up to leaders of denominations, Christian music, Christian literature, and television ministries.

I am inclined to believe those reports. Nothing else explains the overwhelming inundation of New Age beliefs, witchcraft, paganism, etc., into Christianity...as well as the blasphemous statements and practices, homosexuality, rejection of Biblical doctrine, and ecumenism with evil religions.

It's not just happening to Churches and Pastors hooked on numbers growth, but also those obsessed with signs and wonders. And it's happening to Churches where few or if anyone prays, and cold formalism and rituals have replaced a once vibrant spiritual life.

In fact, one Church had demonic people in leadership that had controlled the Church for years. They had had 20 Pastors in 20 years. The Church was a stain in the city.

We are in a very dark and evil period when Christianity is replete with that type of Church and I don't know how some professing Christians and their Churches are going to survive.

The facts are...many Churches, and even some denominations, are in danger of being overthrown by evil people.

I do not know if anyone has a firm grasp on how extensive and deep the infiltration is. From my observations, and the degree of apostasy, I would say that it is a severe infestation."[4]

    Of what? Of real live actual Satanists taking over Churches, denominations, leadership positions all over the place! This is the tactic. And folks, we better wake up and deal with reality! Satan is not only real & has a real evil character but he's really implementing his evil tactics in the Church today by sending his actual evil emissaries right in our midst, Satanists, trying to destroy us from the inside out. It's time to wake up! This is not a game, it's a war! Put on the full armor of God!

The **second way** the devil seeks to destroy the Church is by **Workers of Satan.**

Now we're talking about his desire to infiltrate the Church with witches. As we saw with Satanists, witches too are also increasing all over the country and their numbers are getting so big now, they're even banding together going after our President:

RT News Reports: *"As the White House continues to battle leaks and the media it does appear that some of Trumps critics are resorting to different methods to try to derail his presidency.*

With protests, people marching in the street with their signs against Trump, Donald Trump is a stupid clown, and mockery, as on TV show making fun of President Trump being played by Alec Baldwin, 'Yes, this is real life, yes this is really happening.'

Failing to stop Donald Trump from being the president, it's time to resort to the supernatural. Like the movie Hocus Pocus. A facebook group is calling on witches across the US to cast a mass spell against Donald Trump and last Friday it attracted 12,000 likes. Celebrities are joining in too.

After an instruction manual went viral, telling witches what to throw into their

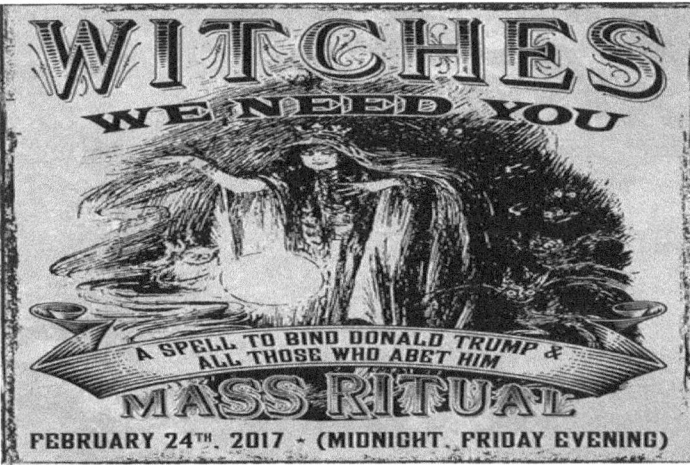

caldron to create the ultimate anti-Trump potion. First thing you need is an unflattering picture of Trump, then not just any color but an orange candle, if you can't find a candle, a baby carrot will do, a Trump Tarot card which will be cast again and again and again on every crescent moon in the month until Trump is not in office."[5]

Now, notice how the media actually picked up on this and reported it, but they also downplayed it with humor and acted like it was a bit of a joke and nothing to worry about. It's only a fringe group of people. Not so! Witches have not only increased on a massive scale in our country, as we saw before, but now their tactics are going beyond just casting spells against the President of our country. Now they're coming into the Church. Why? Because we don't believe in them anymore. Haven't you heard? It's just a figment of our imagination! It's just a scare tactic from Preachers. And so again, they too, just like Satanists, get to sneak in under the radar without notice in the Church in our midst tearing things apart, destroying things, dividing us up into little pieces, like this next report shows.

REPORT OF WITCHES INFILTRATING CHURCHES

"Several high-profile Pastors have urged me to put into print what we now know, in order to alert the Church to some of the dangers we are now facing.

We now know of a large number of Churches that have been successfully infiltrated by witches. In fact, in one town, witches boast that they have infiltrated every Church in the town and judging by the devastation caused in some of the Churches in this town, their claim is probably correct.

Their plan is meeting with amazing success. One Church that we have been told of, originally had a membership of well over 100. The membership is now down to 30 and the remaining members are almost totally demoralized.

This is now happening to an increasing number of Churches and many promising young Pastors are now leaving the ministry because of it.

These witches are working to a carefully laid out plan which has been operating for many years, right under our noses without our even suspecting it. Some profess to be fine Christians. They dress well, speak well, are usually well educated and in some cases, are knowledgeable in spiritual matters.

Some witches appear content to just sit in congregations and mumble their incantations while others go out of their way to gain acceptance in a Church and then carefully work their way into positions of influence. In fact, one high priest successfully got himself elected as Secretary of a Baptist Church.

They become members and begin to take an active part, singing in the choir or joining the diaconate etc. Then they work to a highly effective plan which is aimed at destroying the Pastor's reputation (seducing him or spreading rumors about him).

They also create factions within the Church and pit one group against another and thus create division. They may lay charges against the Pastor and put these charges in writing and send them to the diaconate. This ploy often divides members of the diaconate against each other or sometimes turns the diaconate against the Pastor.

Witches can cause a 'heavy, oppressive atmosphere' in a meeting, so that people feel 'tired' and cannot concentrate on the message. This 'oppression' can only be removed by the Lord's people praying against it...otherwise the 'heavy' atmosphere will remain.

Witches can send demons into Churches to disrupt worship services and prayer meetings. They can set Christians against each other by gossip and slander. They can break up Christian marriages and can easily demoralize weak Christians and cause them to fall away.

The results stemming from these methods are obvious and manifold - confusion, suspicion, loss of confidence in the Pastor, emotional problems, tension, disunity – the list is almost endless, and we are certain that this is only the tip of the iceberg.

Unfortunately, the Church in these last days has become so worldly and materialistic, that it is no longer any real threat to its enemies.

I constantly hear Christians talk about 'spiritual warfare' and 'putting on the armor of God' etc., but it would appear that with most, their knowledge of these things is theoretical rather than experimental. They are familiar with the 'jargon' but that is as far as it goes."[6]

In other words, these people have no clue what they're up against and they're getting slaughtered! But folks, this is real. Real live actual witches are taking over Churches, denominations, leadership position all over the place! And we better wake up and deal with reality! Satan is not only real and has a real evil character, but he's really implementing his evil tactics in the Church today by sending his actual evil emissaries right in our midst, witches, destroying us from the inside out. Why? Because we no longer believe in him! Haven't you heard? He's just a figment of your imagination…a scare tactic from Preachers. When the whole time, this is a tactic from satan to get us to allow him right in our very midst, to infest us and destroy us, taking us out! We better wake up! We're in a war not a game! Put on the full armor of God.

The **third way** the devil seeks to destroy the Church is by **Possessors of satan.**

And what we're talking about is how he seeks to infiltrate the Church with fake Christians who are demonically possessed. But that doesn't happen does it? Yeah right! I've had to deal with this so many times in ministry I've lost count! The Bible is clear, folks. Not everybody who goes to Church services is saved. They might really be a fake phony Christian, which means they could possibly have a demon in them:

BIBLICAL EVIDENCE OF FAKE CHRISTIANS

DEAD FAITH BELIEVERS: James 2:14,17 "What good is it, my brothers, if a man claims to have faith but has no deeds? Can such faith save him? In the same way, faith by itself, if it is not accompanied by action, is dead. You believe that there is one God. Good! Even the demons believe that – and shudder."

DEAD ATTENDANCE BELIEVERS: 1 John 2:19 "They went out from us, but they did not really belong to us. For if they had belonged to us, they would have remained with us; but their going showed that none of them belonged to us."

DEAD RELIGION BELIEVERS: Matthew 7:21-23 "Not everyone who says to me, Lord, Lord, will enter the kingdom of heaven, but only he who does the will of my Father who is in heaven. Many will say to me on that day, Lord, Lord, did we not prophesy in your name, and in your name drive out demons and perform many miracles? Then I will tell them plainly, I never knew you. Away from me, you evildoers!"

DEAD BEHAVIOR BELIEVERS: Titus 1:16 "Such people claim they know God, but they deny him by the way they live. They are despicable and disobedient, worthless for doing anything good."

FALSE BROTHERS: (Greek - pseudadelphos – a false brother, one who in a showy way professes to be a Christian but is destitute of Christian piety or knowledge.)

Galatians 2:4 "This matter arose because some false brothers had infiltrated our ranks to spy on the freedom we have in Christ Jesus and to make us slaves."

2 Corinthians 11:26 "I have been constantly on the move. I have been in danger from rivers, in danger from bandits, in danger from my own countrymen, in danger from Gentiles; in danger in the city, in danger in the country, in danger at sea; and in danger from false brothers."

FALSE LEADERS: (prophets/teachers, etc.)

Matthew 7:15,16 "Watch out for false prophets. They come to you in sheep's clothing, but inwardly they are ferocious wolves. By their fruit you will recognize them."

2 Corinthians 11:13 "For such men are false apostles, deceitful workmen, masquerading as apostles of Christ."

2 Corinthians 11:14-15 "And no wonder, for satan himself masquerades as an angel of light. It is not surprising, then, if his servants masquerade as servants of righteousness. Their end will be what their actions deserve."

2 Peter 2:1-2 "But there were also false prophets among the people, just as there will be false teachers among you. They will secretly introduce destructive heresies, even denying the sovereign Lord who bought them – bringing swift destruction on themselves. Many will follow their shameful ways and will bring the way of truth into disrepute."

Well how could that happen in the Church? Because people in the Church don't believe in satan anymore and they don't understand his evil character and they don't really believe he'd really have an evil tactic to send fake, phony, even demonically possessed, people into the Church to destroy it even in leadership positions when it's going on in a massive scale! We already saw demon possession is increasing all over the country, just like with witches and satanists but now there's so many of them, people possessed, they're coming into the Church. Don't believe me? Let's listen to this next report:

PEOPLE POSSESSED INFILTRATE THE CHURCH

"A man named Joe, not his real name, had a normal education and then found employment. In his late teens and early twenties, he became associated with others who used to conduct séances.

After some time, Joe became a medium himself and developed the ability to call up spirits. The spirit world was completely new territory to Joe and the power he developed began to frighten him, so he backed away. He found new friends and occupied himself in other ways.

Eventually, he met a very nice young lady and they were married. They were invited by some friends to accompany them to a Church service. They were counselled that night and showed every evidence of being born again but the Church they went to was one where so-called speaking in tongues was practiced by most of the congregation.

Joe wondered what to make of the strange mutterings that went on all around, after all, he had never witnessed this in any of the Churches that he had attended in his younger days. It seemed to have some close affinity with what he had observed in his encounter with spirits back in those séances.

A few weeks later, Joe was talking to 'Bill Smith' (not his real name) in the parking lot outside their Church. Joe says, 'That new deacon who was elected recently, he's not fit to be a deacon. His car was seen late one night outside of 'Mrs. Widow's home'.

Bill Smith was a bit shocked, but he could not deny what Joe was saying because, well, maybe it was true! Mrs. Smith, on being told by her husband of this conversation, could hardly wait to get on the phone to tell this 'juicy' bit of gossip to others.

The end result was that 'Mr. New Deacon's' wife heard about it and that caused a somewhat strained relationship between her and her husband.

Bill Smith decided to take Joe aside and ask for an explanation, only to find that Joe strongly denied having made such a statement.

Then another time, Joe is talking to Mr. 'Old Member' and says "I think we should have a change of Pastor; after all, it's not good for a Church to have a Pastor who has been divorced!"

Mr. 'Old Member' is stunned for he didn't know their Pastor had been divorced. After all, that was not mentioned when the Church extending him a call.

By this time, few people were enjoying the services. The atmosphere seemed 'heavy' and no one seemed able to concentrate. Most people were totally mystified by the recent developments.

No one could really understand why Joe continued to lob his verbal grenades with devastating effect on the congregation and then remain completely oblivious of all the shock waves that rolled over them.

The whole fellowship had changed from a warm caring group, to now a cold, untrusting congregation. A spiritual damper had been thrown over the whole congregation.

Now what has really happened in this Church? Satan has set this Church up - 'set-up' for destruction! In a way too clever in fact to be 'human'. It has been set up supernaturally!

Joe has demons! They gained entry to him when he became a 'medium' in his younger days and when he was 'slain in the spirit' that spirit world door was opened even wider.

And now Joe became a tool, with the demons now being able to destroy the work and witness of a good evangelical Church without anyone knowing it.

We must understand that satan is a master strategist. Until fairly recently, his tactics seem to have been more of a 'diversionary' nature.

However, they have now changed to that of 'infiltration'. The enemy is ... NOW IN OUR MIDST and often appears as an 'angel of light' and even some of his servants are appearing as 'ministers of righteousness'.

Had we understood the Scriptures better, we surely would have expected this in these last days.

And now large numbers of Christians have lost their biblical balance and do not see demons as being responsible for anything. They see corruption, crime, violence, immorality and all kinds of perversion and just accredit it all to human nature, just something natural.

But the stark fact is, the forces of darkness are now clothing themselves in human form and sitting in our congregations, singing in choirs and working in various departments of our Churches."[7]

I've dealt with this in every Church I've ever Pastored. I've had people from a family of generational witches serving on the Church board. I've had a lady who professed being a Christian who literally within days went from one ministry to the next causing division, fighting, disruption, on to the next because people kept kicking her out, and then she turned on me when I began to administer discipline. I had another guy who went after a newly saved Christian girl and all of a sudden, he shows up out of the blue wanting to date her, and he said all the right things, had the Christian jargon down, said he loved the Church. Then it came out he was involved in the occult and had an altar at his house. And even here in Las Vegas we've had people, all of a sudden, cursing in the middle of services, interrupting prayer in the services, causing distractions during services, and getting up and down going in and out of the facilities right when the altar is given. You really think that's by chance? Folks, we need to wake up and get our head out of the sand. Satan is not only real, but he's really sending his evil emissaries, even demon possessed people, right into our midst, to take us out! And it's much more common than you think, as this man shares:

"I was preaching a revival in a small Church of about 100 people and people were coming and being saved. And one night, after the altar call, a man came in whom I had not seen before.

He certainly had not been in the building during the preaching. He was going about laying hands on people. Before I could get to the Pastor to ask him about the man, an old lady, with her hair in a bun, absolutely beaming with the presence of the Holy Spirit, walked up to the man.

She had her Bible clutched in her right hand and said, 'Mister, don't you know that God's people know when we've got a devil amongst us?'

Then she swung and smacked him in the head with her Bible. He was stunned but didn't move fast enough. She hit him again. In fact, she hit him several times before he navigated through the crowd and made it out the front door on a dead run.

The point is this, Churches with godly people committed to God, praying, studying the Bible, do not get infiltrated. They recognize the one in whom Satan had an influence through a demon. There is no soft entry point for them and they could not remain as an attendee.

And so, if there is going to be any purging of a Church today, or any other sector of Christianity, the people of God have to get serious about knowing God.

I'm not saying that I advocate smacking the infiltrator with a Bible. But I am saying that if we are not dedicated enough so that we can discover the many truths of God, how are we going to recognize the emissaries of Satan?

The very continuance of Christianity depends on how well professing Christians understand and react to this truth. This is not a game! It is a life or death struggle for the eternal destiny of souls!"[8]

Wow! That sounds like battle language. Where have I heard that before? But folks, we need to deal with this reality. Demon possessed people, along with Satanists and witches, are coming into the Church today because we no longer believe they exist! Haven't you heard? He's just a figment of your imagination, a scare tactic from Preachers, when the whole time this is a tactic from satan to get us to allow him right in our very midst, to infest us and destroy us, taking us out! It's time to put on the full armor of God! In fact, when you're a mighty strong Christian, or a mighty strong Church, the enemy can't touch you, as this former devil worshipper shares:

John Ramirez grew up in the Bronx, where his relatives practiced witchcraft. *"My father's side of the family were witches and warlocks. My father was very heavy into Santarea, into spiritualism. I was not only answering to my mother and my father, but I was also answering to the demons."*

John's involvement with Santarea deepened quickly. "I was being taught and trained by high ranked devil worshipers into spiritualism. When drug dealers got killed in the street I wanted to run out there and get human blood to do witchcraft. I'd light up my candles, I'd spit the rum, I'd blow the cigar smoke because the cigar smoke means power.

If I didn't have money for the blood I would cut myself and use my own blood and pour it in. The atmosphere in the room changes. You know there's something there.

When you know they are there you must address them like a family member. 'My father, I'm here, what would you like to speak to me about. What is it you want me to do?'"

As time went on John also practiced the dark arts outside his apartment. He preyed on Christians in particular. "At the clubs, I would go around looking for Christians. I knew in clubs, it was a devils' playground.

So, I knew if I could get in and you already had a beer or two in your system, I knew all I had to do was say, 'Hey I have something to tell you today.' And that person would say, 'What is it you want to tell me?' And that's the gateway."

Eventually John became a high priest. A form of African spiritualism. As he became more powerful John took warfare more seriously. "The Devil told me I had to go into the neighborhood in the spirit realm in order to weaken it in the natural. Whatever you can kill in the spirit realm you can kill in the natural.

So, I would leave my body home and astral project myself to different regions, different cities, different states, different countries. As I would go through neighborhoods I would speak curses, speak things that I wanted to happen to the neighborhood.

Sometimes I would go into a neighborhood and I would see people on the corner praying holding hands, heads bowed, praying up a storm. I knew there wasn't anything I could do in that neighborhood. That neighborhood was sanctified, blessed, through prayer, you couldn't touch it. But in the other neighborhoods it was party time."[9]

In other words, he had a heyday with them. Why? Because they were fake, there was no substance. They weren't true godly on fire Christians or Christian Church, and so they got chewed alive by the devil! When are we going to wake up and realize that contrary to the skeptical Church today, satan is real and he's alive and well on planet earth and he's really spreading his evil tactics right here among us! We need to take this seriously! We're not in a cakewalk Christian! We're in a war! This is not a game. This is a serious battle mission from God. Put on the full armor of God. But again, if you're reading this today and again, you're not saved, you need to realize that the devil already has you and you're fair game. He can mess with you any way he wants! If that guy wanted to put a curse on you and kill you he could! You have no protection as a non-Christian. You better get saved now!

But Church it's time to get our head out of the sand and stop being ignorant of the devil's schemes! There's a war going on and it's not just abroad but its right here in our own country. It's a cosmic battle for the souls of men and women all around us. The stakes are high, and millions of lives are at risk. If we're ever going to win this war, then the American Church needs to once again shine for Jesus Christ and take this seriously! This is no time to be Denying the Tactics of Satan! We need to Wake up Church! The alarm has sounded. We are under attack, it's the satanic War on the Christian. Don't let the enemy get you! Amen?

Chapter Six

The Tactic of Demons

"It was your average morning with people heading off to work, kids walking to school, and toddlers riding their tricycles, under their mothers' watchful care. But all that was going to change in the blink of an eye.

At 2:00 AM that very morning, a plane carrying its deadly cargo called, 'Little Boy' began its historic mission.

And as expected, the ground radar detected incoming aircraft, but since there was no sign of bombers, the people on the ground thought the danger had already passed. Therefore, the plane continued on.

In fact, exactly one hour later the radar again spotted two B-29's and issued yet another warning for the people to head for shelter. However, the people ignored it because they thought for sure that this was just another false alarm.

And so, precisely sixteen minutes later, Little Boy was dropped and unlike his name he left behind a massive mushroom-shaped cloud near the center of this thriving city.

The destruction was instantaneous and unbelievable, with 90% of the buildings being obliterated by 1,000 mph winds.

And the loss of life was absolutely inconceivable with 140,000 people being incinerated by temperatures above 9000 degrees Fahrenheit.

The year was 1945. The plane was the Enola Gay. The bomb was atomic. The city of course, was Hiroshima."[1]

Now folks, how many of you guys heard of the Bombing of Hiroshima? I think most of us have. And how many of you guys would say that the bombing of Hiroshima was one of the worst disasters of all time? But with all due respect to those who lost their lives in the Bombing of Hiroshima, what if I were to tell you that I know of a disaster that makes the bombing of Hiroshima look like a mere firecracker? And what if I were to tell you that this disaster didn't occur in just one place, and one country, at one time, but it's going on right now today all over the world and it's been leaving a trail of death and destruction for centuries. I'm talking once again about the *Satanic War on the Christian*. And the facts are these. We Christians don't battle here and there once in a while. We go to war, every single day. Whether you see it, feel it, believe it or not, the moment you got saved you entered a spiritual war against a demonic host whose sole purpose is to destroy you and extinguish your testimony for Jesus Christ. And what's wild is that most wars go on for a few years or even longer. But *the Satanic War on the Christian* has been going on for the last 2,000 years non-stop and it's sending people straight into hell! Most people will readily talk about all the other wars throughout history and all their atrocities, and rightly so, we have the History Channel. We need to talk about them! Yet how many people, even Christians, will openly discuss the longest war in mankind's history. The *Satanic War on the Christian* that has destroyed more lives than all the wars put together?

Therefore, in order to stop getting duped and beat up all over the place, we're going to continue in our study, The *Satanic War on the Christian*.

Now so far, we've seen if you're ever going to win a war, then **the first thing** you must do is **Know Who Your Enemy Is**.

The **second thing** is you need to know is **What Your Enemy is Like**, their character, amen? It's common sense, right?

And last time we saw **the third thing** you need to know is **The Tactic of Your Enemy.**

What they're up to, what's their goal, why are they here, why are they doing what they're doing? Why in the world are we in a war in the first place? We saw the tactics of satan are NOT good. In fact, he's very methodical about his evil attacks! He literally schemes to destroy us in three different ways. He infiltrates us, the Church, with Followers of satan or Satanists, workers of satan or witches, and even possessors of satan, actual demon possessed people to come in and take us out! This is serious stuff and it's really going on! It's not a scare tactic of preachers to get your money. It's Satan's tactic to destroy us! But, that's not all.

The **second tactic** we need to deal with if we're going to stop getting beat up and duped all over the place as Christians, in This *Satanic War on the Christian* is **The Tactic of Demons.** Satan is not the only one scheming to infiltrate the Church and destroy us with his methodical attacks.

So are his evil horde of demons that aid him in his evil attacks against us. They too have their own tactics out to get us!

Luke 4:31-37 "Then He went down to Capernaum, a town in Galilee, and on the Sabbath, began to teach the people. They were amazed at His teaching, because His message had authority. In the synagogue, there was a man possessed by a demon, an evil spirit. He cried out at the top of his voice, 'Ha! What do you want with us, Jesus of Nazareth? Have you come to destroy us? I know who you are – the Holy One of God!' 'Be quiet!' Jesus said sternly. 'Come out of him!' Then the demon threw the man down before them all and came out without injuring him. All the people were amazed and said to each other, 'What is this teaching? With authority and power, He gives orders to evil spirits and they come out!' And the news about Him spread throughout the surrounding area."

Here we see when Jesus was preaching the Word of God and doing so with great authority, what happened? A demon possessed person created a ruckus in their midst. And, where were they? In the synagogue! Not in the world! Not in some back alley or creepy occult book store. But right smack dab in the middle of a synagogue! And can I tell you something? The same thing is happening in the Church today!

Now, this is not Christians being possessed because as we saw before, a Christian can't be possessed. Therefore, this man was obviously not saved but he did have a demon. And there he was in their synagogue service, right there in their midst, and when the Word of God was being preached and Jesus was being magnified and a demon manifested itself! That's exactly what we see going on in the Church right now. Satanists, witches, and demon possessed people really are going into Churches to take them down.

Now I said all that to get to this. Here's my point. Satan is not the only one behind these infiltrations. Demons too have the same tactic as satan and they're working with him to infiltrate the Church today and destroy it as well. The first way demons are seeking to destroy the Church is by promoting a new service. They twist things around, so they can grab control. You see, demons not only want to come in to your Church service as we saw last time, in the last days, but they want to control it so they can eventually destroy it. But let's remind ourselves about what Church services are to be about.

Colossians 3:16-17 "Let the word of Christ dwell in you richly as you teach and admonish one another with all wisdom, and as you sing psalms, hymns and spiritual songs with gratitude in your hearts to God. And whatever you do, whether in word or deed, do it all in the name of the Lord Jesus, giving thanks to God the Father through Him."

I don't know how you can get any clearer than this, but according to the Bible, our Church services should be all about Who? Hello! God, right? What does it say there? It's all about Him! We not only teach His Word and sing songs of gratitude to Him, but whatever you do, it's all for His glory, right?

But not anymore! Haven't you heard? Christianity is getting a little too boring and we need to spice things up a bit, get some good entertainment going on around here, you know what I'm saying? That'll bring people in! And lest you think no one would fall for this demonic tactic, you tell me if this is not the attitude of the average person that comes to Church services today? It has nothing to do about God. It's all about them, right? You cater to my needs. It's all about me, me, me…I want to be entertained! Make me feel good!

Here's my point. Where in the world do you think that mindset came from? Who do you think put that idea in their head? And who do you think is getting Churches to cater to it? That's the problem. It's not only not Biblical, hello, our services are supposed to be about the glory of God, but the problem is this behavior opens Pandora's box. Once you start going down this route, of catering your services all around self instead of the Savior, you just opened the floodgates of Apostasy as well as demonic deception! Anything can come in! Don't believe me? Check out all these "new and improved" self-pleasing entertaining Church services, and you tell me if demons don't have control.

Beer Drinking Service: Most Christians are familiar with the Biblical story of Jesus turning water into wine, but now two New Zealand Pastors are seeking to turn a pub into a church complete with beer-drinking during the gatherings. While the sports bar service will not contain any sermons or singing, the Pastors say it will serve as both a place of prayer and a place to grab a beer. And they're not the only ones. Another Pastor in California is doing the same thing. "Some Churches use tactics like providing coffee and sweets, but a new church in San Jose has a very different approach. It provides beer for attendees. Pastor Jenkins said this is where the real ministry takes place. 'Come on," he says, 'I'll buy you a pint!"

Tattoo Parlor Service: A Michigan pastor who says he's doing everything he can to reach out to people who don't feel comfortable at a traditional house of worship has opened a tattoo parlor inside his church. Rev. Steve Bentley said his ministry is built on the belief that mainstream religion has become ineffective and irrelevant to most people. To that end, he opened Serenity Tattoo.

Brian Brown is the manager of Serenity Tattoo Studio, a Bridge Ministry, in Flint Township. He never imagined he'd work at a tattoo parlor in of all places, a church. Tracy can't imagine going anywhere else to get her tattoo. As he is in the process of tattooing Tracy's' shoulder she says, "It feels good to come in here, I know it's a nice, safe, environment". Being home to a tattoo studio isn't the only thing unique about this church. They also host MWO wrestling events and later this year they plan to bring in cage fighting.

The Holy Ghost Hokey Pokey Service: If you not only want some good ol' fashioned entertainment at your next Church service, but a free healing to boot, you can attend this Church and join them in a "new" movement of God called the Holy Ghost Hokey Pokey.

Preacher says, *"Three weeks ago we did a Friday night Holy Spirit, and we saw 12 people speak the word of knowledge and 40 healed during the Holy Ghost Hokey Pokey. Let's just go ahead and do that and see what the Lord does. Are you guys ok with doing the Holy Ghost Hokey Pokey?" The crowd watch as the music leader comes up on stage and is handed the mic. "OK Brian is going to lead us in the Holy Ghost Hokey Pokey."*

Brian proceeds to lead the crowd in song, *"Put your right hand in, put your right hand out, put your right hand in and you shake it all about"*. As he gets further into the song, and the crowd is doing what the song says, the music gets louder, the crowd is having fun and they start yelling with the music while waving their hands all about over their heads. When the song is over certain members of the crowd start coming forward to testify of what has just happened to them while singing and dancing to the Holy Ghost Hokey Pokey.

The first person comes forward and says, "When I started doing the Hokey Pokey, with the arms I had no effect, but when I started doing the legs, you put your right foot in and out and then the left foot in and out, I could feel in my knees that all of a sudden I had no pain."

The Can-Can Dance Service: One Church service included a lady who said the Spirit of God gave her the "Left Leg Anointing". Suddenly she kicks up her left leg (like the "Can-Can" dance), and says, "More Jesus", whereupon people are supposedly slain in the Spirit in the direction of her kick. Then she proceeded to take the Lord's name in vain saying, "Oh my God, Oh my God, Oh my God", which she later changes to "Oh my goodness."

The Hiss Like a Snake Service: Another Church service included the so-called minister hissing like a serpent and sticking his tongue out grunting loudly as he walked through the crowd. And all the while in the background people are yelling, screaming and making animal sounds.

The Squeal Like a Pig Service: Go to this service and you would have heard the sounds of pigs squealing and while people are dancing a jig.

The Moo Like a Cow Service: Or go to another service and you'd see a lady "mooing" like a cow with two so-called ministers rolling around on the floor beside her.

The Baa Like a Sheep Service: Or go to this service and you join these folks "baaing" like a sheep.

The Bark Like a Dog Service: Or for those of you "canine" lovers out there, maybe you can go to this service and join everyone in barking like dogs. That's right…Who let the dogs out!

The Roar Like a Lion Service: Or if a dog bark isn't loud enough for you, you can go to this Church service whereupon you will be encouraged to roar like a lion.

The Cluck Like a Chicken Service: Believe it or not you can go to a Church service where the so-called minister doesn't preach another boring sermon from the Bible. No! He stands around clucking like a chicken!

The preacher is standing in front of his congregation. With microphone in hand he begins to speak. "OK now, before we go surfing, let's get the reading done. Luke, Luke," Then he laughs. "Chapter Twoooooo," He is putting on a show while reading the scripture and the crowd is laughing. "I tell you 'all, let's look at Chapter one. Cock-a-doodle-doooooo. Elias was a member of the '*again sounding like a chicken*' cock-a-doodle-dooooooo." The congregation listens intently and laughs at all his antics while performing his sermon.

The Toking the Holy Ghost Service: If animal noises just aren't your thing and you really want that "spiritual high," then look no further than these Churches who encourage you toke the Holy Ghost."

"What is Toking the Holy Ghost? This is Toking the Ghost." He puts his finger together as if hold a joint of Marijuana and imitates breathing in the smoke. Then he pretends he is blowing it all back out. Then he explains, *"Toking the Ghost is simply putting your fingers together like you are smoking a joint, but instead of smoking an illegal substance that is harmful for the body, you are inhaling the Holy Ghost with the act of putting your fingers together that looks like you are smoking a marijuana cigarette but in fact you are receiving imparkation from Almighty God. I challenge you today that toking the Holy Ghost is the idea from the Holy Ghost to disturb the religious stronghold, to disturb religious demons, to destroy religious spirits from Hell and get the Church into the freedom and the law and liberty of Christ Jesus, so that you may, two things, glorify God, and enjoy Him."*

Then we hear from members of the congregation. "This is the Springs of Living Waters Church. I am here with John". John says, "I firmly believe in Toking the Ghost. Right, have a little Johovajuana. It's religious and it's free. You reach in your pocket and it's there. You just put your fingers together and breath in. A little whiff of the Glory and then you exhale." "I am just going to give you a little second hand right through the videos screen, all right? Time and space is not an issue, this is a Heavenly realm. So, you just access point right here," as they both put their fingers together and take in deep breaths and then blow it out. They both laugh and say, "There is no high like the Most-High". Another tells us, "Hi out there in internet land, I was just going to...." Then he blows into the screen.

"I was just going to take a big old Glory injection off my baby Jesus. I have taken a baby Jesus and strapped him to a syringe." He holds it up, so you can see the little baby doll that is taped to the syringe. "And I'm just going to take a Glory injection in my veins on the main line, to get some of that good heavy liquid juice pumping through my veins from Heaven. So, here I go." And he injects the whole syringe into his arm.[2]

Maybe it's just me but, I don't think Jesus came all the way from heaven to die a horrible death on the cross, just so we can sit around in our services drinking beer, getting a tattoo, walk around clucking like chickens or smoking a so-called Holy Spirit joint, you know what I'm saying? You talk about blasphemous! And so, here's the point! I don't doubt one iota that these people are having a great time at these so-called Church services, but it's not for the glory of God, which means it's not just not Biblical, its demonic! It's fake, it's phony and it's step one of demons, not just coming into your Church, but taking control of it, so they can destroy it!

The **second way** demons are seeking to destroy the Church is by **Promoting a New Savior.**

Huh? Haven't you heard? The old-fashioned Jesus is getting a little too boring too, and we need to make Him more relevant for our world today, you know what I'm saying? That'll bring people in! And you might think, "Nobody's going to fall for this demonic tactic. Come on! They wouldn't even go so far as to replace Jesus, would they?" Uh yeah, they already have. But let's first get acquainted with the real Jesus.

Revelation 4:8 "Each of the four living creatures had six wings and was covered with eyes all around, even under his wings. Day and night, they never stop saying: "Holy, holy, holy is the Lord God Almighty, who was, and is, and is to come."

1 Peter 1:15 "But just as He who called you is holy, so be holy in all you do; for it is written: "Be holy, because I am holy."

According to our text, if there's one attribute that God clearly wants us to know about Him, it's what? He is Holy, Holy, Holy, right? And if there's one thing He wants us to know that He expects from us it's what? We are to be holy just like Him, right? Like Father like son, we're His children! But not anymore! Haven't you heard? That's old fashioned. That's outdated! That's not relevant. Thanks to the tactic of demons, in these last days, we are now being told we need a new and improved "Savior" that's conformed to our image. I mean, that old Jesus is just way too Holy. People can't connect with that! Therefore, we need a new and improved Savior that's just like us, full of sin and accepts every sin.

Now again, lest you think no one would fall for this demonic tactic, you tell me if this is not the attitude of the average person that comes to Church services today. It has nothing to do about Jesus or His Holiness or the holiness He expects from us His people! There's no talk about sin, His hatred of sin, His wrath, or repentance and the need to escape from hell. It's all about come one, come all, no matter who you are, what you do, non-repentant sin and all! In fact, they've even gone so far as to condone sin openly in the Church! Don't believe me? Check out all these "new and improved" Savior Church services, and you tell me if the demons aren't grabbing control!

The Pole Dancing Savior: *"Here's a new way to express your faith. On the second Sunday of every month, Crystal Deans leads a pole dancing course for church-goers in Texas. She says she knew exotic dancing wasn't for her, but she realized she could use her experience with exotic performing to help other women connect with the teaching of Jesus Christ."*

Fox News Reports: *"I bet you have never heard of this one before. 'Pole Fitness for Jesus'. You're probably thinking how on earth could you mix pole dancing with Jesus. Well, according to one studio, you can definitely mix the two. The dancer proceeds to tell her students, 'You are going to step in front, with your inside leg next to the pole, and kick the other leg around the pole.' She proceeds to tell us, 'I was a dancer for three years, about 7 years ago. I did it for a while.*

It was not something that I felt very rewarded with. But to each his own. It was just something I didn't want to do anymore. So, I decided to take the part that I actually liked about that and bring it here.'"

Reporter: *"Don't let the name of the class fool you though, there's no prayer before hand, and no crosses hanging in her studio. She says, 'Just to get past the whole stigma, I teach women how to feel good about themselves, I teach them to be empowered and we get into really good shape. I mean it does the legs, that's why we wear the shoes.'"*

The Erotic Church Service Savior: *"Hundreds lined up for a new Erotic Church service where a female dancer danced in a skin colored stocking in the middle of the church facility in front of the altar. Nearly one thousand interested people waited outside the door despite a thunderstorm. Above the entrance was the caption, "A warm welcome to the Vineyard of Love". Then a man came to the microphone and announced, "This is an erotic church service, can you move a bit closer together, all of you." This was followed by saxophone music and dance. Then it was announced that, "eroticism and lust are not taboo pushed aside by God." In fact, "lust has to be lived out." Then the faithful were asked to take part in an anointing ritual in which they should massage the forehead and hands of the person sitting next to them. And one congregant stated, "This is how church services should be." Then they all said, "Our Father" together and then were encouraged with these words, "Praise God with your body, your lust and tenderness." And judging by the enthusiastic applause, the audience fully intended to do this."*

Transgender Pastor Savior: *"The Episcopal Church's House of Bishops on Saturday approved a proposal that, if it survives a final vote, would give transgender men and women the right to become ministers in the church. The move comes nine years after the Episcopal Church approved its first openly gay bishop, sparking an exodus of conservative parishes. The church now allows gay men and lesbians to join the ordained ministry and the new resolutions on gender would now allow transgender individuals as well." It's all part of their overall non-discrimination policy to church members."*

The Adultery Approving Savior: *"One Church Bishop warned that all this ongoing redefinition of marriage with same sex unions will soon include the idea of what's being called, 'non-monogamy' or the concept of faithfulness between a man and a woman in marriage being outdated. The new concept will be the* *acceptance of 'multiple partners' without the stigma of adultery. In fact, a court case has already been brought forth claiming that since same-sex marriage restrictions are being lifted, so should restrictions on multiple-partner marriages."*

The Atheist Accepting Savior: *"Believe it or not, there's now a new 'ministry' being offered to the Church. Jerry DeWitt, a Pentecostal Preacher for 25 years, now turned atheist, is encouraging other atheist pastors to stop pretending like he did and 'come out' and admit their atheism. He's the executive director of what's called 'Recovering from Religion' and its slogan is, 'Thousands of organizations will help you get into religion, but we're the only one helping you out.' One person stated, 'It wouldn't be growing if there wasn't a need for it,' which tells you the status of the American Church.*

In fact, this so-called "ministry" of people "recovering" from Christianity is not only for Pastors, but now it's for any so-called Christian. A psychologist from Berkeley is helping former fundamentalist Christians to lose their religion in a workshop called, 'Release and Reclaim.' "Their God was a capricious, vindictive, punishing figure. Now, they need help learning to trust themselves."

The New Age Occult Savior: *The Church of England has recently hosted a 'New Age Festival' where it opened its doors to tarot card readers, crystal healers, meditation experts, and dream interpreters. The Church is in trouble and attendance has fallen for the sixth year in a row, so they decided to hold the festival in a bid to embrace alternative forms of Christianity. But this shouldn't be surprising because another Church leader has stated that, "Harry Potter is a Christ-like figure because he promotes Biblical values, and a Protestant church in California teamed up with a high priestess of the pagan fertility goddess Isis to help them with "guided meditations" in their fifth annual "Faith and Feminism Conference." The high priestess stated, "I've taken people to their past lives in Egypt, as that culture had all the secrets. They're the ones that knew." I mean, gee whiz, what's next? A full-blown "new age" Church service?*

"Namaste," A Hindu gesture of greeting or farewell. "I am the spiritual leader of the Loving Spirit Community," says Gene Ferrara, "We have opened a center, a center for conscience living. There we do a variety of events during the course of a week. Starting with Sunday morning, what we call 'A Celebration of Life,' we do some chanting, some singing, some honoring of the spirit in each other, I get to do my little metaphysical rant. Then we do a guide in meditation. Allowing

people to come on an inward journey that I facilitate." During his service, he is saying to his group as they are meditating, "Feel yourself emerging from this darkness which has become light. Once again into a universe of swirling colorful energy." They are humming, and a flute is playing in the background. "The function here is to encourage and inspire people to awaken to their true nature, their spiritual nature so they can incorporate that perspective and that point of view into their daily lives to make their human experience more meaningful and joyful."[3]

    I don't think Jesus came all the way from heaven to die a horrible death on the cross, so we could sit around having Erotic Church Services, while our palms are getting read, saying a Hindu farewell, you know what I'm saying? In fact, for those of you who don't know what "Namaste" means, it's the Hindu way of saying, "I bow to the god in you." You're acknowledging the other person is a god. What? You talk about blasphemous!

    And once again, here's the point! I don't doubt one iota that these new so-called Saviors are pleasing to sins of man, but that's not the Real Jesus! He is Holy, He is Holy, He is Holy! And He has zero tolerance for sin, which is why He had to die on the cross for us! Which means these "new and improved" saviors can't save a thing, which means they're useless, they're dead…they're demonic! It's a last days tactic of demons to not just come into your Church, but to destroy it!

    And speaking of which, demons and New Age Church services, what I'm about to share with you, I've had for several months now, and now I want to show it to you in this context. I'm going to share with you a picture of two guys, taken at a Church service in Arizona, and I only show it to you because I know where it came from directly, firsthand, and it's not some Photoshop trick on the Internet. You can't trust that stuff out there, but this is not that case. This so-called Church service, where this photo was taken, it just happens to be a so-called Church that's getting into all this fake Jesus, New Age, self-seeking type service mentality. What I'm going to show you is that this mentality apparently not only helps demons to feel so comfortable in your Church service, but to even walk around in your midst.

    A lady named Christine took the photo on the following page on her iPhone of a young man on the left side, (light gray jacket) and her husband is sitting next to him (red t-shirt) immediately after this Church service had ended. She took the photo in April and forgot about it. Four months later in August, the young man in the gray jacket was killed. He was shot at point blank range as he was answering a knock on his front door. Although the police never apprehended his killer, they believe it was someone he knew from his past. He had been involved in drugs. When Christine found out that their friend had been murdered, she wanted to help his family. They didn't have any current photos of him. She remembered the photos she had taken of him on her cell phone and she gave them to the funeral home, so they could be used for his service.

That's when Christine was approached by the funeral director and began to ask her questions regarding the photos she had taken and wanted to know who took the photos, what device was used and the location where the photos were taken. Christine answered her questions, but she asked the funeral director why she asked. The funeral director told Christine it was because of the image she had captured on one of the photos. Christine relooked at the photo and had no idea what she had captured walking around in the background of this so-called Church service. Christine was shocked. She had absolutely no idea that she had captured, apparently, a demon. She was carrying around the photo and didn't even know it. In fact, if you zoom in you can see even more details.

These are the same kind of things I used to see before I got saved and was involved in the occult. But I say all that to get to this. Where is this demon walking around, having a good ol' time? Not in an occult book store, or a satanists meeting, or witches coven, but a so-called new and improved Church service with a new relevant savior that accepts all sin. We need to wake up and get our head out of the sand.

Demons are not only real, but they're so comfortable in these Apostate Churches today, that they're walking right out in the open, ready to destroy us and take us out!

The **third way** demons are seeking to destroy the Church is by **Promoting a New Experience.**

You see, they not only want to come in to your Church service, and walk freely about in your Church service, they ultimately want to come inside of people and possess them in the Church service. It's the ultimate step of destruction. Just like the guy in the synagogue, full blown demon possession, this is now going on in the Church today. And they're doing it by promoting a new form of worship. I mean, haven't you heard? That traditional form of worship is boring! And we need to spice things up a bit! That'll bring people in! And lest you think nobody would fall for this demonic tactic, let's first get acquainted with true Biblical worship. How it's supposed to be.

Ephesians 5:17-20 "Therefore do not be foolish but understand what the Lord's will is. Do not get drunk on wine, which leads to debauchery. Instead, be filled with the Spirit. Speak to one another with psalms, hymns and spiritual songs. Sing and make music in your heart to the Lord, always giving thanks to God the Father for everything, in the name of our Lord Jesus Christ."

The Bible says that one of the best things you could ever do with music is to what? We are to praise God with it, right? And this is why every time we gather together, as the Church, we are to sing songs to God not ourselves that are God-glorifying, God-honoring, and God-exalting. Why? Because we are so in love with Him, and we're so thankful for what He's done for us, we can't help but sing love songs back to Him, right? That's the purpose of Christian music!

Not Anymore! Thanks to the tactic of demons, in the last days, we are now being told you've got to gut all your songs of the Name of Jesus and switch to generic terms, like He or Him. Why? Because the world doesn't like to hear song after song about God and Jesus and the Bible? I mean, what are you trying to do, run them off or something? That's bad marketing. Remember, it's all about the numbers. You need to sing songs that they like, and that fit their style and their preferences, and man you keep that up…listen…you're going to have numbers coming out of your ears! Huh! Isn't that what makes for a successful Church today? And then on top of that, haven't you also heard? People don't want to come and learn at a Church service today and think and study, no, they want to feel an emotion, have an experience, you know what I'm saying? And man, if you can combine that with your music, you got something! Yeah, something alright, a demonic lie! I'm telling you, this has become the latest "craze" in so-called worship. Gut it of everything that has to do with Jesus, God, and the Bible, and spice up that emotion to the inth degree!

But my question is, "Just who are you worshipping?" You never mention the name of Jesus. You only say He or Him. And so, I'm left wondering what is that? Are you singing about your boyfriend, your fiancé, your husband? Who's he? Why don't you mention the Name of Jesus? This is a Church service! Hello! We're supposed to be singing songs to Jesus! What's wrong with that? Personally, as I've shared before, I think it's a spiritual warfare issue! Put yourself in the shoes of a demon, the last thing you'd ever want to hear people singing in the Church is the Name of Jesus, right? Why? Because that's the only Name by which people can be saved and that's the only Name that can cast you out of this place you're so stinking comfortable in, and I'm talking about the Church! So, demons are whispering into people's ears that a true, spiritual, on fire, Christian, in these last days, is one who can let it all hang out! You know, things like jumping up and down, screaming and shouting, swaying back and forth, dancing and going crazy and wild! Whoo! See how spiritual you are! Surely that's from God, right? No! It's demonic. It's supposed to be about Jesus!

Let me state it again on record that I don't have a problem with showing emotions during a Church service! Although I admit, if one of our interns got up here and started rolling around on the floor, we'd have to lay hands on him. But seriously, I don't believe that clapping is illegal or that raising your hands will invite the judgment of God! I do wonder if we're ever going to clap on time but that's another point. But seriously folks, that's not what's going on here. These expressive emotional encounters we're being told to demonstrate our spirituality and gut everything of Jesus, it's counterfeit!

In fact, it's a classic technique to get people into an altered state of consciousness so they can be possessed by a demon. Don't believe me? Let's take a look at how the occult gets people demonically controlled:

"During these sessions, in the very strange environment, people speak in tongues, they yell, and they scream, they talk in foreign languages, it's like a mad house, it's real crazy, everyone bounces around on foam pads, fly up into the air." Says one of the attendees.

Rajneesh is one of India's most controversial gurus largely because of his endorsement of shocking sexual practices as a prerequisite for salvation. His brand of Yoga called Dynamic Meditation, is a New Age combination of Hinduism and psychotherapies. This exercise involving rigorous breathing and hyperventilation, is designed to arouse the serpent force called Kundalini, which the gurus believe lies coiled at the base of the spine. The next phase of Dynamic Meditation is screaming, it feels like you finally had an opportunity to throw a tantrum as a little kid. By the time you get to the third phase, of jumping up and down and yelling who, you are hardly there at all. And it's pretty hard to remember what happens once you are there. I guess the closest thing I can associate it with is mindlessness. You get to a place where your mind actually leaves your body. Your body is just jumping up and down and the voice from your gut is yelling who, you're not doing it any more. You become one with this whole energy.

The next phase in Dynamic Meditation is quiet space. Someone yelled stop and you have been doing 30 minutes of intense catharsis and what happens after being in such an incredibly intense movement for so long is just a feeling of peacefulness and stillness. My mind actually stops, and I feel a oneness with the whole universe."[4]

Hmmm. So that's how the occult gets people worked up into an altered state of consciousness…jumping up and down, swaying back and forth, yelling, to link them with another spirit and "connect" with the universe, so to speak. Let's now look at some behavior that's being encouraged in the Church today and you tell me if there's not a strange parallel:

HINDU SERVICES VS. SO-CALLED CHURCH SERVICES

FIRST PHASE: The Hindu followers first began with a form of "repetitive movement" combined with "music" for an extended period of time.

Some Church services today include people "repeatedly" running around, jumping up and down, swaying back and forth, etc. to the beat of so-called "worship" music.

SECOND PHASE: The Hindu followers then started to speak forth a "repetitive phrase" or "mantra" over and over again until it became mindless.

Some Church services today include people speaking forth a "repetitive phrase" or a so-called "unknown language" over and over again.

THIRD PHASE: The Hindu followers then started to "shout repeatedly" over and over again as a way of further "releasing" themselves from reality.

Some Church services today include people "shouting, yelling, screaming" over and over again in order to "let it all hang out" in their so-called "worship" of God.

FOURTH PHASE: The Hindu followers finished this occult mind-altering procedure with a sudden ceasing of all activity so as to "feel" a connection with the universe or spirit world.

Some Church services today include people being requested (after a prolonged period of repetitive movement, repetitive speaking, repetitive shouting) to then be completely still and silent so as to "feel" the so-called presence of the Holy Spirit.[4]

Yeah, you feel the presence of the spirit alright, but it ain't the Spirit of God! Your services are not God-honoring at all. It's a demonic deception. I don't doubt these people are having an emotional encounter with something, but again, it's not the Spirit of God. In fact, they might actually have just gotten possessed by a demon! It's the same occult technique the Hindus use! And again, what we're talking about here is 'non-Christians' who go to Church services. Does that ever happen? Yeah, as we saw before. It's rampant in the American Church. A Christian can't be possessed. So, if you see a person in the Church being possessed by another spirit other than the spirit of God, they're not a Christian no matter what they say, okay? And for those who think that could never really happen in the Church, people getting full-blown demonically possessed, let's take a look at what this behavior leads to.

KUNDALINI (SERPENT) SPIRIT IN THE CHURCH

"Andrew Strong, Author of Kundalini Warning tells us the following: I want to show you some of the shocking things and just how similar they are to the

Kundalini cults of Hinduism and the New Age movement, Eastern religions. The stuff that's been invading for the past 16 to 17 years, I believe is the worst invasion in Church history.

It became known as the Toronto Blessing went worldwide under that name. Nobody knew what that was about. People falling down, acting drunken, laughing hysterically, shaking uncontrollably, jerking backwards and forwards, they're heads going back and forth, some people roaring like lions, people making animal noises, this stuff had never been seen in a church on this scale before. And it invaded worldwide.

So, all around the world, especially in the commonwealth countries, like England and all through the UK, Australia, New Zealand, Canada and many other nations all over the world. The Charismatic movement was into this stuff for the largest part, so this thing became a worldwide sensation just in a couple of years.

Now the basic question we are asking is why these manifestations are so similar to Eastern Religions and Hinduism and the Kundalini cults and yet they're not found in scripture, found in the Bible, they're not found in Biblical Christianity at all.

Of course, in Hinduism, the most common ways of experiencing a Kundalini awakening is through a guru placing his hand on your forehead. When they do that you will be infused with this incredible love and this wave of emotion, you will fall down, there will be all these manifestations, animal noises, joy and weeping, and shaking, this is a kundalini awakening and amazingly, it is exactly the same as we have been seeing in the Toronto Blessing.

Now one of the very clearest signs of a Kundalini awakening has always been kriyas. A woman can be walking along, and she will have these involuntary jerking motions. The staggering thing about it is that we are seeing again and again and again these same types of kriyas right through the Toronto movement. This has always been one of the clearest signs of Kundalini that we know of.

A friend of mine from South Africa who has done a tremendous amount of research on this topic says that Kundalini is like a false Holy Spirit. It produces miracles and even healings, visions of love and power and emotion and all these kinds of things and yet it is a Hindu version of the Holy Spirit and it's not holy.

It's the same as you watch Faith Healers on TV as they touch a person and that person falls to the ground or jerk around the floor as they fall to the ground uncontrollably, some as if they are having seizures."[5]

Wow! Just like in the synagogue 2,000 years ago, people in the Church being demonically possessed. Why? Because that's the Last days tactic of demons to destroy us! Folks, we need to wake up and get our head out of the sand and realize that demons are not only real but they're really invading the Church spreading their evil tactics right here among us! We need to stop being ignorant of their schemes, just like the devil! There's a war going on and it's not just abroad but its right here in our own country. It's a cosmic battle for the souls of men and women all around us. The stakes are high, and millions of lives are at risk. If we're ever going

to win this war, then the American Church needs to once again shine for Jesus Christ and take this seriously! This is no time to be Denying the Tactics of demons! We need to Wake up Church! The alarm has sounded. We are under attack, it's the satanic War on the Christian. Don't let the enemy get you! Amen?

How to Receive Jesus Christ:

1. Admit your need (I am a sinner).

2. Be willing to turn from your sins (repent).

3. Believe that Jesus Christ died for you on the Cross and rose from the grave.

4. Through prayer, invite Jesus Christ to come in and control your life through the Holy Spirit. (Receive Him as Lord and Savior.)

What to pray:

Dear Lord Jesus,

I know that I am a sinner and need Your forgiveness. I believe that You died for my sins. I want to turn from my sins. I now invite You to come into my heart and life. I want to trust and follow You as Lord and Savior.

                        In Jesus' name. Amen.

Notes

Chapter 1   *The Existence of Satan*

1. *The Battle of Normandy*
   (https://en.wikipedia.org/wiki/Invasion_of_Normandy)
   (https://www.britannica.com/event/Normandy-Invasion)
   (http://www.ddaymuseum.co.uk/d-day/d-day-and-the-battle-of-normandy-your-questions-answered)
2. *People's Beliefs on Satan*
   (http://www.nytimes.com/1997/05/10/us/is-satan-real-most-people-think-not.html)
   (http://www.christianpost.com/news/most-u-s-christians-don-t-believe-satan-holy-spirit-exist-38051/)
   (Video – From the show The View – Source Unknown)
3. *Little Girl Acting Like the Devil*
   (https://www.youtube.com/watch?v=VfEYyNxQc7o)
4. *Proof of the Rise of Satanism*
   (http://www.telegraph.co.uk/news/religion/8416104/Surge-in-Satanism-sparks-rise-in-demand-for-exorcists-says-Catholic-Church.html)
   (http://www.onenewsnow.com/legal-courts/2010/08/17/schools-claim-lucifer-as-model-and-guardian)
   (http://archives.onenewsnow.com/Perspectives/Default.aspx?id=724962)
   (http://www.tampabay.com/news/bizarre/florida-man-tells-county-let-me-pray-to-satan-or-dont-pray-at-all-before/2250957)
   (http://www.weeklystandard.com/satanic-black-mass-to-take-place-tonight-at-harvard/article/791269)
   (https://www.vice.com/en_us/article/xd5gjd/heres-the-first-look-at-the-new-satanic-monument-being-built-for-oklahomas-statehouse)
   (http://www.tulsaworld.com/news/capitol_report/satanic-monument-headed-for-oklahoma-or-arkansas-to-be-unveiled/article_5c2ec8c3-880a-5a5b-b9da-973af6c31f87.html)
   (http://cw39.com/2015/10/09/greater-church-of-lucifer-set-to-open-in-old-town-spring/)

(https://vigilantcitizen.com/latestnews/the-satanic-temple-unveils-a-massive-statue-of-baphomet-in-detroit/)
(http://www.theblaze.com/news/2014/09/18/satanists-reveal-plan-to-join-atheists-in-battling-bibles-at-public-schools-and-take-a-look-inside-their-controversial-satanic-coloring-book/)
(http://www.dailymail.co.uk/news/article-2556446/The-sickening-smile-teen-accused-satanic-ritual-murder-15-year-old-girl-kidnapped-raped-bashed-death-lid-toilet.html)

5. *Why People Get into Satanism*
   William C. Wiser, *The Darkness Among Us*,
   (Nashville: Broadman & Holman Publishers, 1994, Pgs. 13-20)
6. *Where Satanist's Meet*
   William C. Wiser, *The Darkness Among Us*,
   (Nashville: Broadman & Holman Publishers, 1994, Pg. 133)
7. *When Do Satanist's Meet*
   (http://www.theopenscroll.com/hosting/SatanicCalendar.htm)
   (https://www.dailystrength.org/group/satanic-ritualistic-abuse-support-group/discussion/satanic-holidays-warning-may-trigger)
8. *What Satanist rituals Look Like*
   William C. Wiser, *The Darkness Among Us*,
   (Nashville: Broadman & Holman Publishers, 1994, Pgs. 180-182)
9. *Testimony Satan Can't Touch Christians Without God's Permission*
   (https://www.youtube.com/watch?v=I11L71PD3Lw)

Chapter 2   *The Existence of Demons*

1. *Story of the Battle of Gettysburg*
   (https://en.wikipedia.org/wiki/Invasion_of_Normandy)
   (https://www.britannica.com/event/Normandy-Invasion)
   (http://www.ddaymuseum.co.uk/d-day/d-day-and-the-battle-of-normandy-your-questions-answered)
2. *The Size of a Roman Legion*
   (https://en.wikipedia.org/wiki/Roman_legion)
3. *Media Making Fun of Demonic Activity*
   (https://www.youtube.com/watch?v=VA1nhSujbz4)
   (https://www.youtube.com/watch?v=aGb8pMIeY6w)
4. *The Origin of Demons*
   Russell L. Penney, *Equipping the Saints Discipleship Manual*,

(Fort Worth: Tyndale Biblical Institute, 1997, Pg. 88)
5. *The Location of Demons*
   Russell L. Penney, *Equipping the Saints Discipleship Manual*,
   (Fort Worth: Tyndale Biblical Institute, 1997, Pg. 88)
6. *The Identity of Demons*
   (http://www.biblesprout.com/articles/hell/demons/)
   Merrill F. Unger: *Biblical Demonology*,
   (Grand Rapids: Kregel Publications, 1994, Pgs.40-
7. *Third World Demon Possession*
   (https://www.youtube.com/watch?v=iSdJJN4z_kQ)
8. *Modern Day Demon Possession*
   (https://www.youtube.com/watch?v=G0uLqh65A8g)

Chapter 3   *The Character of Satan*

1. *Battle of the Buldge*
   (https://www.britannica.com/event/Battle-of-the-Bulge)
   (http://www.history.com/topics/world-war-ii/battle-of-the-bulge)
   (https://en.wikipedia.org/wiki/Battle_of_the_Bulge)
2. *Character of Satan*
   H. Wayne House, *Charts of Christian Theology & Doctrine*,
   (Grand Rapids: Zondervan Publishing House, 1992, Pgs. 79-80)
   (http://www.allaboutgod.com/names-of-satan-faq.htm)
   (https://bible.knowing-jesus.com/topics/Satan,-As-Deceiver)
   (https://www.gotquestions.org/names-of-Satan.html)
   (http://www.markbeast.com/satan/names-of-satan.htm)
   (https://bible.org/seriespage/6-survey-bible-doctrine-angels-satan-demons)
3. *Quotes on the Power of the Media*
   (http://adage.com/century/rothenberg.html)
   (http://adage.com/news_and_features/special_reports/tv/1960s.html)
   (http://www.uoguelph.ca/~mbateson/principles.html)
   (http://cana.userworld.com/cana_occultTerms2.html)
   (http://www.cuttingedge.org/news/n1385.cfm)
4. *Sex and violence in the Media*
   (https://www.focusonthefamily.com/lifechallenges/love-and-sex/purity/what-your-teens-need-to-know-about-sex)
   (https://www.sagepub.com/sites/default/files/upm-binaries/23151_Chapter_6.pdf)

(http://screenrant.com/10-tv-shows-most-nudity/)
(https://en.wikipedia.org/wiki/Nudity_in_American_television)
(http://www.vulture.com/2014/08/cable-nudity-countdown-clock.html)
(https://en.wikipedia.org/wiki/Virgin_Territory_(TV_series)
(http://www.mtv.com/shows/virgin-territory)
(http://deadline.com/2014/07/happyland-incest-mtv-craig-zadan-neil-meron-802510/)
(CNN Broadcast – Married & Dating? Ad Campaign by Pro-Adultery Site – YouTube Video – Source Unknown)
(http://www.cyfc.umn.edu/Documents/H/K/HK1005.html)
(http://www.cyfc.umn.edu/Documents/C/D/CD1001.html)
(http://www.cyfc.umn.edu/Documents/C/B/CB1032.html)
Ted Baehr, The Media-Wise Family,
(Colorado Springs: Chariot Victor Publishing, 1998, Pg. 19, 70, 71)

5. *How Much Money is Spent on a Super Bowl Ad*
(https://www.si.com/nfl/2017/01/26/super-bowl-commercial-cost-2017)

6. *Sex & Violence in our Behavior*
(http://atlanta.cbslocal.com/2014/10/06/cdc-110-million-americans-have-stds-at-any-given-time/)
(https://www.cdc.gov/std/stats14/std-trends-508.pdf)
(http://www.nbcnews.com/health/health-news/ongoing-severe-epidemic-stds-us-report-finds-f1C8364889)
(http://articles.latimes.com/2012/jan/19/news/la-heb-teen-pregnancy-20120119)
(http://www.nytimes.com/2012/02/18/us/for-women-under-30-most-births-occur-outside-marriage.html)
(http://www.nytimes.com/2012/04/15/opinion/sunday/the-downside-of-cohabiting-before-marriage.html)
(https://economix.blogs.nytimes.com/2010/08/28/birthrates-marriage-rates-and-divorce-rates-fell-in-2009/)
(http://www.telegraph.co.uk/travel/maps-and-graphics/mapped-countries-with-highest-divorce-rate/)
(http://www.ipsnews.net/2017/02/the-rise-of-one-person-households/)
(http://www.fatherhood.org/fatherhood-data-statistics)
(https://rstudio-pubs-static.s3.amazonaws.com/109737_8b2d5f8d1c0442449623a4191e03042b.html)
(http://www.gallup.com/poll/3163/majority-considers-sex-before-marriage-morally-okay.aspx)

(http://www.gallup.com/poll/8839/outofwedlock-births-morally-acceptable.aspx)
(http://www.gallup.com/poll/1651/gay-lesbian-rights.aspx)
(http://www.nydailynews.com/news/crime/stabbings-reported-pennsylvania-high-school-article-1.1750425)
(http://www.sandiegouniontribune.com/sdut-florida-teen-accused-of-poisoning-teachers-drink-2014mar13-story.html)
(http://www.dailymail.co.uk/news/article-2332522/Man-puts-week-old-daughter-freezer-stop-crying-faces-life-bars.html)
(http://www.nbcnews.com/NbcNews_2014/news/crime-courts/california-women-arrested-after-3-children-found-starving-1-chained-n59516)
(http://www.insideedition.com/headlines/11933-mom-who-killed-son-by-injecting-hand-sanitizer-into-his-feeding-tube-gets-40-years)
(http://abcnews.go.com/US/florida-couple-arrested-abandoning-kids-woods/story?id=22769212)
(http://cleveland.cbslocal.com/2014/02/01/police-grandmother-forced-feces-covered-underwear-down-11-year-old-granddaughters-mouth/)
(http://www.clickorlando.com/news/caregiver-used-stun-gun-to-punish-kids-kissimmee-police-say)
(http://pittsburgh.cbslocal.com/2014/01/24/couple-headed-to-trial-for-driving-with-son-in-trunk/)
(http://abc7chicago.com/news/police-mom-kills-8-week-old-son-in-apparent-murder-suicide/1511125/)
(http://www.reuters.com/article/us-usa-texas-infant-idUSBREA0E0WE20140115)
(http://nypost.com/2014/01/24/dad-killed-kids-after-slaying-wife-because-he-didnt-have-car-seats-for-mexico-trip/)
(http://www.reuters.com/article/us-usa-texas-murder-idUSBREA081JF20140109)
(http://www.nbcmiami.com/news/local/Pregnant-Woman-Blames-Hormones-For-Attack-on-Roommate-Deputies-239641111.html)
(http://www.nbcmiami.com/news/North-Miami-Beach-Man-Fatally-Shot-After-Fight-Over-Utensils-Breaks-Out-at-Baptism-Party-239260151.html)
(http://www.browardpalmbeach.com/news/florida-man-bites-neighbors-ear-off-over-a-cigarette-6454471)
(http://www.nbcdfw.com/news/local/Woman-Stabbed-for-Bringing-Home-Pizza-Instead-of-Chicken-239757201.html)

7. *Harry Potter Kids Quotes*
(http://www.youtube.com/watch?v=745X5b5qniM)

8. *Witchcraft in Military Services*
   (KENS 5 San Antonio News Broadcast – Witches Amon Us/San Antonio's Military Witches – YouTube Video – Source Unknown)
9. *Lady turned into Vampire*
   (https://www.youtube.com/watch?v=Z127wKKWfXg)
10. *Paganism is on the Rise*
    (http://www.youtube.com/watch?v=-6UBO7IOStA)
11. *Wicca is Fastest Growing*
    (http://www.apologeticsindex.org/w03.html)
    (http://www.christianpost.com/news/online-witch-school-wicca-fastest-growing-religion-59799/)
    (http://thetruthwins.com/archives/the-fastest-growing-religion-in-america-is-witchcraft)
12. *Trailer of New Show Called Lucifer*
    (https://www.youtube.com/watch?v=X4bF_quwNtw)
13. *Show Childhoods End Promotes Devil as a Good Guy*
    (https://www.youtube.com/watch?v=Rr25OLacsdc&list=PLcbo3s7XSa876YEqrGDa_OMcaGxudu4xS)
14. *Man Wants to Look like the Devil*
    (https://www.youtube.com/watch?v=iLpruZuFQDM)

Chapter 4   *The Character of Demons*

1. *The Battle of 1812*
   (http://www.history.com/topics/war-of-1812)
   (https://www.marinersmuseum.org/sites/micro/usnavy/08/08a.htm)
   (https://en.wikipedia.org/wiki/War_of_1812)
   (https://www.britannica.com/event/War-of-1812)
   (https://en.wikipedia.org/wiki/The_Star-Spangled_Banner)
2. *Character of Demons*
   H. Wayne House, *Charts of Christian Theology & Doctrine*, (Grand Rapids: Zondervan Publishing House, 1992, Pgs. 77,79)
   (https://bible.org/seriespage/6-survey-bible-doctrine-angels-satan-demons)
3. *Rise of Drug Use*
   (https://learnaboutsam.org/wp-content/uploads/2016/11/SAM-report-on-CO-and-WA-issued-31-Oct-2016.pdf)
   (http://www.nbcnews.com/health/health-news/pot-fuels-surge-drugged-driving-deaths-n22991)

(http://thechart.blogs.cnn.com/2011/09/08/study-22-million-americans-use-illegal-drugs-3/)
(https://www.usnews.com/news/blogs/data-mine/2015/08/19/the-heroin-epidemic-in-9-graphs)
(https://www.cdc.gov/drugoverdose/data/heroin.html)
(https://www.upi.com/blog/2013/10/11/Super-potent-new-form-of-meth-found-in-Texas/7501381524829/)
4. *Pat Robertson and the Church of Marijuana*
(https://www.theguardian.com/commentisfree/cifamerica/2012/mar/12/pat-robertson-marijuana-message)
(https://www.youtube.com/watch?v=HW3lvOKucR0)
(https://www.youtube.com/watch?v=6s4Jgj7u3xs)
5. *Dave Hunt Drugs Ticking Off Neurons in Brain*
(https://www.youtube.com/watch?v=h4zn_Z-7Zt4)
6. *Flakka Demon Possession*
(https://www.youtube.com/watch?v=X-N2LwJL75g)
7. *Statistic on Drug Usage*
(https://www.sciencedaily.com/releases/2013/06/130619132352.htm)
(http://www.cbsnews.com/news/study-shows-70-percent-of-americans-take-prescription-drugs/)
(http://blog.centerforinnovation.mayo.edu/2015/12/15/popping-pills-a-drugged-nation/)
(http://www.wnd.com/2014/02/70-million-americans-taking-mind-altering-drugs/)
(http://www.businessinsider.com/painkillers-kill-more-americans-than-heroin-and-cocaine-2012-9)
(http://www.cbsnews.com/news/us-leads-the-world-in-illegal-drug-use/)
8. *Prescription Drugs Cause Killings*
(https://www.youtube.com/watch?v=02eXgWyMLY0)
9. *Psychiatric History & Drug Abuse*
Matthew Olson, *An Introduction to Theories of Personalities*,
(Upper Saddle River: Prentice Hall, 1999, Pgs. 20, 23, 47, 48, 65, 66, 67, 70, 129, 502)
(http://www.wayoflife.org/fbns/jung.htm)
(http://philipcoppens.com/jung.html)
(http://www.psychoheresy-aware.org/psych_briefs.html)
(https://thepsychologist.bps.org.uk/volume-21/edition-1/when-therapy-causes-harm)
(http://www.wordofgodtoday.com/psychology-bible-2/)

(http://www.openculture.com/2014/04/igmund-freud-researched-got-addicted-to-cocaine.html)
(https://www.sonoma.edu/users/d/daniels/horneylect.html)
(http://www.users.miamioh.edu/shermalw/honors_2001_fall/honors_papers_2001/scheer_horney.htm)
(http://www.encyclopedia.com/topic/Abraham_H_Maslow.aspx)
(http://www.cchr.org/)

Chapter 5 *The Tactic of Satan*

1. *Attack on Pearl Harbor*
   (http://www.historyplace.com/worldwar2/timeline/pearl.htm)
   (http://en.wikipedia.org/wiki/Pearl_Harbor)
2. *Tactics of Satan*
   H. Wayne House, *Charts of Christian Theology & Doctrine*, (Grand Rapids: Zondervan Publishing House, 1992, Pg. 78)
3. *Former Satanists Invade Church*
   https://www.youtube.com/watch?v=0RNijNuvrBQ
4. *Satanist invading Church*
   http://www.truthkeepers.com/?p=982
5. *Witches praying against Trump*
   https://www.youtube.com/watch?v=Up1w7Ywb26M
6. *Witches infiltrating Churches*
   http://www.christianissues.biz/pdf-bin/brycehartin/thelastdays.pdf
7. *People possessed infiltrate the Church*
   http://www.christianissues.biz/pdf-bin/brycehartin/thelastdays.pdf
8. *Demon Possessed in Church*
   http://www.truthkeepers.com/?p=982
9. *Enemy Can't Curse Christians*
   https://www.youtube.com/watch?v=6l7A4cQHxuY

Chapter 6 *The Tactic of Demons*

1. *Story of Hiroshima*
   (http://en.wikipedia.org/wiki/Atomic_bombings_of_Hiroshima_and_Nagasaki)

(http://www.wtj.com/archives/hiroshima.htm)
2. *The New and Improved Self Church Services*
    (http://www.christianpost.com/news/new-zealand-pastors-create-sports-bar-church-service-complete-with-beer-drinking-79293/)
    (http://www.christianpost.com/news/california-church-preaches-gospel-at-the-bar-beer-replaces-coffee-59980/)
    (http://news.yahoo.com/pastor-opens-tattoo-parlor-inside-michigan-church194456243.html)
    (http://www.fox10tv.com/dpps/news/strange_news/pastor-opens-tattoo-parlor-inside-michigan-church-ob12-tvw_4033498)
    (http://www.bible.ca/tongues-audio-video-documentation.htm)
    (http://www.tzemach.org/articles/torbless.htm)
    (https://www.youtube.com/watch?v=vTPowYQ-jVU)
    (https://www.youtube.com/watch?v=pxunCIEI-18)
    (Toking the Ghost – John Crowder – YouTube Video – Source Unknown)
3. *The New and Improved Savior*
    (http://www.aolnews.com/2011/03/25/former-exotic-dancer-crystal-deans-teaches-pole-dancing-for-Jesus/)
    (http://www.thebereancall.org/content/hundreds-queue-erotic-church-service)
    (http://articles.chicagotribune.com/2012-07-07/news/sns-rt-us-usa-religion-transgenderbre8660ix-20120707_1_first-openly-gay-bishop-episcopalians-gene-robinson)
    (http://www.wnd.com/2011/07/320969/)
    (http://religion.blogs.cnn.com/2012/06/13/unbelieving-preachers-get-help-to-come-out-as-open-atheists/)
    (http://books.gather.com/viewArticle.action?articleId=281474977005360)
    (http://www.dailymail.co.uk/news/article-1370694/Church-England-row-cathedral-opens-doors-tarot-card-readers-crystal-healers-new-age-festival.html)
    (http://www.telegraph.co.uk/culture/harry-potter/8083870/Harry-Potter-is-Christ-like-claims-theologian.html)
    (http://www.wnd.com/2011/10/360365/)
    (New Age Church Service/Pastor – YouTube Video – Source Unknown)
4. *Parallel Hinduism and Church Service*
    (https://www.youtube.com/watch?v=5i6PBui-bN8)
5. *Kundalini Serpent Spirit Awakening*
    (https://www.youtube.com/watch?v=WfXmDkQiE2o)

www.ingramcontent.com/pod-product-compliance
Lightning Source LLC
LaVergne TN
LVHW091304080426
835510LV00007B/379